A Candle in the Darkness

The Dave Sikes Story

By Andrew H. Knef

(Front cover illustrated by Judy McClure, Freelance Illustrator-Writer & Artiste Extraordinaire, New Baden, IL)

National Library of Canada Cataloguing in Publication

Knef, Andy
A candle in the darkness / Andy Knef ; illustrated by Judy McClure.
ISBN 1-4120-0149-8
I. Title.
PS3611.N44C35 2003 813'.6 C2003-902452-0

TRAFFORD

This book was published *on-demand* in cooperation with Trafford Publishing. On-demand publishing is a unique process and service of making a book available for retail sale to the public taking advantage of on-demand manufacturing and Internet marketing. **On-demand publishing** includes promotions, retail sales, manufacturing, order fulfilment, accounting and collecting royalties on behalf of the author.

Suite 6E, 2333 Government St., Victoria, B.C. V8T 4P4, CANADA
Phone 250-383-6864 Toll-free 1-888-232-4444 (Canada & US)
Fax 250-383-6804 E-mail sales@trafford.com
Web site www.trafford.com TRAFFORD PUBLISHING IS A DIVISION OF TRAFFORD HOLDINGS LTD.
Trafford Catalogue #03-0517 www.trafford.com/robots/03-0517.html

10 9 8 7 6 5 4 3

Author: Andy Knef - an award winning writer, journalist and healthcare professional with over 20 years of experience. He is employed at BJC Health Systems in St. Louis, MO as the manager of Creative Services.

TABLE OF CONTENTS

Dedicated to our daughter, Kerri

Foreword

By The Rev. Gene Neff, Director of Ministry to the Sick and Aged for the Catholic Diocese of Belleville

In recent years, studies have been conducted at Duke University by Dr. Harold Koening and colleagues and by the National Institute for Healthcare Research and David and Susan Larson. Results of the studies have concluded that positive spirituality plays an important role in holistic wellness (physical, psycho-social and spiritual) for the individual. Many have tried to define "spirituality." To advance one understanding of spirituality – someone else's or my own – would be presumptuous. For how can we limit "spirituality?" However, there are some common elements in the definitions that have been proposed: relationship, growth and the meaning of life are some. The search for meaning in one's life is that person's spirituality. Positive relationships with a Higher Power, others, oneself and the world around us give life meaning, give life hope.

We can approach life in a variety of ways. Years ago, I hung two posters in my office that reflect opposite views of life. The negative view of life: Life is a bowl of cherries. Why do I get all the pits? The positive view of Life: When someone gives you a lemon, make lemonade."

Dave Sikes' story is the story of a young man who has been given a "lot of lemons." His spirituality has enabled him to squeeze those lemons and make lemonade. In the spirit of St. Francis, every time despair appears at his doorstep, David has been called to make a choice. Each time he draws upon an inner spiritual strength. That spiritual strength included healthy, life-giving relationships with God, his wife and family who love one another, and a will to live life to its fullest within the limitations of (or should I say in spite of) that life. His spiritual strength- his spirituality – continues to give him hope.

The wisdom that Dave teaches us in his responses to suffering is the spiritual significance of meeting responsibilities and having integrity. Dave personifies the maximum, "pray as if everything depends on God. Work as if everything depends on you."" Put the two concepts together and miracles can happen.

While Dave continues to confront physical health issues on his life's journey, his story – as you will read in the following pages – is a story of hope. It is a story of relationships – with God, parents, sister, spouse, children and grandchildren, extended family and helath-care providers – that are life-giving. It is a story of committed service to God, family and country – that is life-giving. It is a story that advocates by, personal example as donor and recipient, the ultimate gift of life – organ donation. And it is the story of suffering. Repeated mental anguish – in Vietman, through a daughter's death, and failing health – would lead many to despair. But for Dave, his spirituality, nurtured and supported by the love of Judy, his wife, has empowered him to overcome despair, grieve the many painful losses in his still short life and achieve an integrity, a wholeness, I call hope.

"A Candle In The Darkness" is a story that challenges us to reflect on our own life's journey and ask the questions: What give meaning to my life? Am I a life-giver, a person of hope? Answering these questions will give you a better understanding of your own spirituality.

The Choice

In the winter of 1995, as Judy drove her husband, Dave, to Barnes Hospital in St. Louis for what she prayed would be a life-saving lung transplant, her mind raced back to another tense drive, to another hospital, four years earlier. As she steered her Ford Probe west toward the Mississippi River, toward the palely illuminated St. Louis Arch and Dave's hoped-for reprieve from a death sentence, the horizon brightened in the February morning chill and Judy's thoughts reversed direction.

The phone was ringing far away. It was Jan. 24, 1991. Dave and Judy had awoken in their Millstadt, Ill., home to a nightmare. A nurse from St. Elizabeth's Hospital in Belleville, Ill., mispronouncing their name "Skies," matter-of-factly informed groggy Judy, "We have your daughter Kerri. She has been in an accident, and we need your permission to work on her." The red digital characters on the Sikes' alarm clock flashed 12:30 a.m.

"Of course, we'll be right there," responded Judy in a calm voice that belied the growing, shrieking panic gripping her heart. "What happened?" asked Dave, abruptly sitting up next to his partner of 22 years.

"Kerri has been in an accident," Judy said. "We have to get to St. Elizabeth's." Dave literally jumped out of bed. A man who measures his sentences carefully at all times, the barrel-chested beer truck driver wordlessly dressed. He stepped out into the clear winter darkness to warm up the family's mini van for the 7-mile trip from Millstadt to Belleville. "I asked the Lord, 'Please don't let her be crippled or badly disfigured,'" he would later recall.

Judy decided to wake the younger of her two daughters, 17-year-old Krista. As Judy stood in her daughter's bedroom door, the usually sound-sleeping teenager startled awake. "Kerri has been in an accident," Judy said without elaboration. Krista, pretty and blond like her 21-year-old sister, threw on clothes furiously. She was extremely close to Kerri, who had always taken her big-sister role as protector and adviser to heart.

The night was crisp and cloudless as the Sikes' — a family lost and alone in their fear and confusion — drove through mostly deserted roads staring straight ahead into darkness. Dave worked to maintain emotional control, driving only a little faster than the speed limit. “I kept thinking how I really didn’t care for the car she had just bought,” Dave remembers today. “It was one of those small convertible jeeps. Even though Judy helped her pick it out, and they liked its sportiness, it didn’t feel solid enough to me.”

Judy remembers uttering a silent prayer, ‘Oh God, don't let her beautiful face be mangled. What if she is confined to a wheelchair?’”

They made the tortuous trip — dissecting southern Illinois cornfields and largely abandoned Belleville city streets — to the hospital in 10 minutes. They left their car in front of the hospital, oblivious to the no-parking signs. They all had the sensation of floating through the front door, somehow detached from their own bodies, unable to hear their own footsteps. They arrived at the admissions desk together.

After taking their names, a nurse led them into a small private room. “The doctor wants to speak to you about your daughter,” she said, softly. The reality of the unfolding horror pushed in on the Sikes. It wouldn’t be held away any longer. “We knew everything wasn’t going to be all right,” Krista recalls.

They waited another five excruciating minutes for the doctor to arrive. Maybe it wouldn’t be the worst, they all hoped. At that moment, a wheelchair seemed like a blessing. The doctor was young, dark-skinned. His slightly accented, methodical speech added to the dream-like quality of the experience. “We did everything we could,” he said slowly. “We weren’t able to resuscitate her. Your daughter is dead.”

The Sikes clung to each other in an involuntary embrace. An invisible fist had punched them all in the stomach. Judy, unable to hold on, fell to the floor. She screamed as if she was on fire. Dave picked her up and they resumed their primordial grope for comfort but there was none in the room, none on earth. Far away, in the background, they heard the faint words of the doctor. He was still talking. He couldn’t be silenced, like Kerri had been. He was saying that Kerri’s friend David had been killed in the same accident. The young man’s parents were waiting in a nearby room.

“Would you be willing to sign a release form to donate her organs?” the physician asked. “She signed the back of her driver's license.” The accumulated weight of the information and pain couldn’t be assimilated. “No,” Judy said furiously, instinctively, finally able to do something to protect her child. “Leave her alone!”

The doctor, unable to grasp the torment around him, got out of its way. "Would you at least consider donating her corneas?" he asked without urgency. "I'll leave you alone to think about it."

No thoughts would come. The Sikes' loss enveloped them like a blanket. They were numb. But gradually, in the silence, amid burning tears and long wordless hugs, Kerri's ever-present smile took shape in their collective thoughts. A thin memory floated into Judy's and Krista's consciousness. Five months before, a happy Kerri had called her mother and sister into her room to witness an act that had clearly pleased the confident young women. "I'm going to sign the back of my driver's license so they can use my organs to help others if I die," Kerri had said with typical finality and determination. "I need you two to sign as witnesses."

Alone now in the hospital waiting room, the remains of a family forged by grief into one vision, left it to Mom to say the words out loud. "It's what Kerri would have wanted. She always wanted to help other people."

The Sikes were sure that the doctor had asked for her corneas because the severity of Kerri's injuries had made her other organs unusable. Judy could see Kerri's bright blue eyes even then: sparkling, full of life, always punctuating a smile.

When the young doctor returned to the room, hesitant to raise the question again, the Sikes told him they had changed their minds. "We'll sign the release, " Dave offered. "Can we see her?"

The decision had helped them all focus. There were more questions now. How did she die? What were the causes? Did she suffer?

The answers brought no relief, just more questions.

The police and responding paramedics estimated that Kerri's blue Geo Tracker convertible rammed into the rear of another car in the center of Highway 15 in Belleville shortly after midnight. Kerri and her young passenger, David, a good friend with whom she shared a passion for music, were returning from a blues concert in St. Louis. Although the driver of the other car wasn't hurt, Kerri's car flipped over, ejecting her and David through the windshield. For that reason, the Sikes would never know if Kerri was actually driving the car. The police found small traces of alcohol in the victim's bodies — well under the legal limit. Kerri's death certificate would say she died of massive internal injuries.

The Sikes are escorted into another room, the room where Kerri died. They believe this because, as they approach the gurney on which she lies, they notice the ventilation tube that had been inserted into her mouth. Her long blond hair is matted with blood. So is her face and clothes. Despite the ever-present blood and the tubes, sister Krista thinks she looks strangely peaceful, as if deeply asleep.

Kerri is wearing a now crimson-stained white shirt she had borrowed for the concert from a girlfriend and former roommate. Her slacks are olive-green. Krista stands on one side of her motionless sister, Dave and Judy on the other. A nurse asks Krista how old she is and the 17-year-old can't understand if she's asking about Kerri or herself. Krista reaches down and touches her sister's blue-tinged fingers.

Unconnected, distant childhood memories flash into Krista's mind. Her assertive big sister had been almost like a second mother to the sometimes shy girl. Krista remembers a time in kindergarten when a classmate took great satisfaction in stealing her dessert every day at lunchtime. Kerri had walked up to the girl and warned her sternly to keep her hands off her sister's brownies. That was all it took. Today, the *former bully and Krista are close friends. Another time when Kerri was 14, she found four $1 bills in a jeans pocket. Without a second thought, she gave the money to Krista. Now, looking down at her sister's tangled, blood-crusted hair, her pale, white face, Krista recalls Kerri showing her how to wear makeup, how to fix her hair. Krista looks over at her parents in their own world of memories and unrelenting pain.*

"She is still warm," Judy thinks, uncomprehending. She reaches down to tenderly kiss Kerri's cheek one last time. "Looking at her laying there so lifeless, so quiet, I thought about the day she was born. She came into the world kicking and screaming — so alive, my beautiful baby — and she lived her entire life with the same amazing spirit and joy for the special quality of each day. Everyone who knew her loved her."

Dave touches Kerri briefly. Like Krista, he has the strange sense that his daughter is just sleeping, will soon wake up so they can drive home together to Millstadt. But Kerri doesn't stir no matter how hard her dad wills it. "I was wishing that I had gotten the chance to eat dinner with her the night before she died," Dave remembers eight years later, tears cascading down his cheeks. "We usually tried to eat dinner as a family, but I had to work late. Kerri always made those family meals special with her loud laugh, her smiles and her stories. After she was gone, even a simple thing like the evening meal would never be the same."

A lifetime of memories holds the shattered Sikes family tenuously intact, like an unbacked puzzle picture suspended in air. "It's time to go," someone says, though they don't know why exactly. They turn away from Kerri, first Dave, then Krista, and finally Judy, who strains to fix her daughter's face in her mind. She wants to lock away every impression of Kerri – even this awful one. In reality, they're in the room with their lifeless daughter for only about five minutes.

The rest of the day was a blur. A brief, awkward meeting with David's parents – the other living victims of the horrible night – offered more unease than comfort. They were equally devastated, equally confused. Their son, like Kerri, loved blues music. Cold and unhearing on a gurney in a nearby room, he would never achieve his dreams either.

The Sikes left the hospital empty in the knowledge that Kerri wouldn't be coming home with them to Millstadt. It seemed as though there was something more they should do, but Dave, Judy and Krista, tired and disoriented, couldn't quite put a finger on it.

Much later, in his bed, in the darkness of his own room, unable to close his eyes despite more than 24 hours without sleep, Dave imagined he was still holding Kerri in his arms. Except, in his grief-wracked mind, it was September 1970 and Dave had just returned to Belleville, Ill., after a year in the killing fields of Vietnam as a U.S. Marine. The 1-week-old baby girl he left behind had taken her first halting steps and learned to giggle adorably while her father became a man and took other men's lives on the other side of the world. Dave joyfully twirled his little girl — blond curls waving — above his head while she laughed. Only Judy fidgeting beside him in their bed, eyes red from crying, brought him back to the inescapable reality of life without Kerri.

Although he didn't fully realize it, Kerri's loss had begun to eat away at Dave in a way that would soon bring him face to face with the toughest life-and-death struggle he had known since his days in Vietnam on patrol with the 1st Reconn Battalion.

Dave in Vietnam, 1970

We Deal in Death

Dave thinks this patrol might be different. The insertion had gone smoother than usual. The huge CH-46 Chinook – after circling low over the landing zone – had abruptly spiraled down to Earth as planned. There was no hostile fire. They had thudded to the earth and piled out the back end ramp with no sign of the enemy at all. Marine Lance Corp. Dave A.C. Sikes had nodded in gratitude at the Cobra helicopter gunships orbiting above in a protective flight pattern.

Now, on the ground, Dave moves out briskly, keeping an eye and ear on the jungle around him. He marks his position relative to his seven Marine Reconn squad mates when he hears a noise that makes the Belleville, Ill., native and married father of one stop breathing.

Corporal Sikes has stepped effortlessly, snugly into a 1-foot-by-1-foot straw-covered hole. Buried in the hole's walls, on each side, are two Chinese-made fragmentation grenades connected by a thin trip wire. The unforgettable sound he hears is the "ping" of two pins simultaneously pulled from the grenades as he steps on the wire – a process that will inevitably lead to a major explosion, the loss of one of Dave's legs and most likely his life.

Except this time, "nothing happens," says Dave. "I'm thinking, 'I'm dead.' I know I have no time to run and I'm realizing in a weird moment of calm that I'm going to be just another statistic. But five seconds, 10 seconds, a lifetime seems to go by, and nothing happens. The grenades are duds, and I'm thinking, for the first time, that I must have a guardian angel."

Ten months earlier, Dave had arrived at San Diego Marine Corps Recruit Depot in February 1969 after the six-hour flight from St. Louis. He met another kind of guardian angel. The task of Dave's DI was to transform the naïve, 19-year-old Midwestern boy — and the other boys who filed into the Quonset Hut barracks — into trained killers. "One guy had his top button unbuttoned and the DI ripped his entire shirt open," recalls Dave. "I was scared to death."

Dave arrived in San Diego as Marine Corps property only after rejecting a chance to join the Army courtesy of his local draft board. Many of Dave's friends and former classmates at Cathedral High School in Belleville were drafted and ended up in the Army. For some that meant Vietnam, but others avoided combat and completed their military tours in comfortable spots like Germany or Spain.

Dave took another option. His next-door neighbor back in Belleville was a Marine recruiter. Dave liked the idea of doing something special, being someone special. He liked the sharp dress uniforms, too, and he thought his young wife, Judy, would like them as well. He wasn't anxious to go to war, but he wasn't willing to avoid that responsibility either.

Dave's entire life and upbringing had brought him to the belief that men lived up to their responsibilities. That duty, honor and country were more than mere words. If he must go to war, he would do so as part of the most elite fighting tradition ever known. Dave was proud to be a Marine.

In 12 weeks of boot camp, he became proficient in a variety of weapons and combat tactics, but he mostly learned about himself, what he could accomplish under pressure. "In the Marine Corps I found out quickly that you didn't ask questions. You just carried out orders. I decided early on that I would try to stay out of the way and keep my nose clean. I prided myself on keeping my rifle, uniform and bunk in top shape.

My goal was to do the right thing and go home on time."

While he developed a few close friends among his fellow recruits, Dave kept mostly to himself. He thought about his pretty blonde wife who was expecting with their first child back at her parent's home in Belleville. Dave discovered that his real best friend in basic training was his M-14 rifle. His ability to use and maintain that gas-propelled, semi-automatic weapon was his only purpose for existence, the Marines constantly reassured him. He knew he was going to Vietnam to destroy the enemy, and despite his easy-going nature and soft-spoken, somewhat shy demeanor, he was ready to kill if he had to.

Dave wasn't quite prepared for the pool-side amphibious exercises in full combat gear that tested the Midwesterner's limited swimming talents. Still, he persevered through this and other daily challenges: 10-mile, full-pack marches, the obstacle course, the verbal abuse, the surprise inspections.

His successful 12-week basic training test actually seemed to Dave to pass quickly. He moved up the coast to Camp Pendleton where the confident new Marine private completed advanced combat training. On the rugged, tree-lined terrain of Camp Pendleton, Dave honed his weapon skills on the M-16 rifle, M-60 machine gun, M-79 grenade launcher and the 45-caliber pistol.

To finish his training, Dave completed 12 weeks of communications school back in San Diego. Summer stretched into fall and Dave longed to return to Judy. San Diego was chilly at night, but the days were nice, he recalls. "I was learning to be a radio man," Dave says. "That was what the Marines called my MOS, my military occupational specialty."

Dave's MOS actually encompassed a basic, yet critical function in the life-and-death struggle of a Marine combat unit. He is the guy responsible for calling in air support when the going gets tough. Dave learned the technical requirements of operating the PRC-25 short wave radio, and he mastered the specifics of military nomenclature and Morse code. Dave welcomed the unique responsibility of manning the radio lifeline for his Marine comrades.

Despite his uncertain future, the peril he was sure to encounter, Dave believed he controlled his own destiny. "I very much thought I was invincible," Dave says without a trace of bravado. "When I flew home from training in California in

September 1969, I thought I could do anything. Nothing could stop me or stand in my way."

Dave may have been ready for anything, but even he couldn't anticipate the torrent of emotion that washed over him as his wife, stomach bulging, awkwardly embraced him at the airport when he arrived home. Kerri was born only days later — arriving herself, crying, healthy, pink and blue-eyed — at Scott Air Force Base Hospital in Belleville on Sept. 11, 1969.

Dave balanced his baby in his broad forearms at the hospital and thanked God for letting him return home in time to hold this little miracle. A few days later, Dave held Judy, as she softly cried in the same strong arms. Dave quietly reassured Judy that he would come back to her and their new baby. She doesn't need to be afraid. She can count on him, as she always has, to come through.

On Sept. 18, just seven days after their daughter was born, Judy watched Dave walk up the ramp and disappear inside the airplane that took him to war in Vietnam.

His flight actually carried Dave from St. Louis to Travis Air Force Base in California, on to Hawaii, to the island of Okinawa, and finally to Da Nang, close to the demilitarized zone separating

North Vietnam from America's allies in South Vietnam "A big group of us on the plane was told to report to the 1st Reconnaissance Battalion. I didn't know who that was, but I found out real quick," Dave says.

What Dave learned is that he would be part of a unit that tempted death routinely. The 1st Reconn Battalion of the 1st Marine Division was tasked with the unenviable job of deploying eight-men patrols to the field to seek out the enemy and report on their location. Deploying from their base at Camp Reasoner, the crack unit's motto was "Swift, Silent and Deadly." The point of their hazardous excursions behind hostile lines was not primarily to engage the enemy in combat, but to remain undetected so that overwhelming force could be called in to destroy their adversaries. As Dave put it: "I learned that — for a Reconn Patrol — combat didn't usually happen when you see them, it's when they see you."

After his short stay in Headquarters Camp with Alpha Company in Da Nang, he got his first taste of combat on a real patrol. "It scared me to death," concedes Dave, who piled out the back end of the Chinook only to realize his first bush insertion was onto a "hot" drop zone, or DZ in Marine short-hand. "Gun fire opened up everywhere as soon as we hit the ground," Dave says. "My lieutenant is screaming at me that we have to get out of here, but we're pinned down flat on our stomachs, not moving and not firing back because we're afraid we'll give away our positions. Meanwhile, the Chinook is leaving with the eight-man patrol we replaced. We spent hours not moving, waiting to get picked off at any moment before the Chinook could get back and extract us."

Dave settled into a routine of patrols as the unit's radio man. He was dubbed A.C. in honor of his revered role as the squad's electronic connection to home base and tenuous protection. The letters were proudly carved out on the butt of his M-16.

A typical patrol lasts 4-5 days, and his unit carried out one a week. His squad of Marines stealthily covered miles of ground by day, walking from sunup to sundown, looking for the enemy. They followed their map and stayed close to the ground, intent on staying invisible. The patrol rested at night, concealed by darkness and jungle so thick it was impossible to see the stars. They were further concealed by camouflage face paint, which the Marines applied every morning to blend into the foliage. "In addition to my radio gear, I wore 50-75 pounds of gear on my back — my rifle, grenades, 20 clips of M-16 ammo, a 45 pistol, pick and a radio," explains Dave.

Fires weren't possible, so no hot food eased the rumblings in their guts as they hunted the enemy. They survived on cold Sea-rations — dehydrated hunks of unnamable meat — and daily quinine pills to fight Malaria. Fear, heat, exhaustion, mosquitoes and moisture were constant companions. "It's no fun when it's over 100 degrees and you're wearing long sleeves and repellent to keep the mosquitoes and leeches off you," Dave recalls with a grimace. "We were constantly wading through creeks and swamps. I still have scars on my legs from the leeches."

When Reconn Marines do sleep — 3 to 4 hours at the most —they were often forced to straddle trees on the steep hillsides where they stopped to keep from rolling off. They covered their heads with blankets in the stifling nighttime heat and humidity to defend against the hated mosquitoes. In monsoon season, when it rained for a month straight, heavy drops pelted their bush hats, denying the Marines precious sleep. Only half asleep on the open ground, in the blackness, they waited for the snap of a twig to reveal disaster. They peered through the jungle for the light of their enemy's eyes. For two-hour shifts, each man stood watch. His mates gathered in a circle for protective cover. Their trust in each other was absolute and unqualified.

"I had come from a part of the country where prejudice was not uncommon," Dave says with the matter-of-fact tone of someone who has lived on the racial dividing line between East St. Louis and Belleville Ill. "I learned in Vietnam to depend on my black squad mates. When they leave you in the middle of nowhere, you have no choice but to get along. It wasn't just a matter of color. We had guys from New Orleans, New York, New Jersey, Chicago and Texas. They had nicknames like Chunky, Red Neck and Red Dog. They spoke with funny accents; they were from different worlds. But in the jungle at night, waiting for the darkness to light up with gunfire, or someone to sneak in and cut your throat, you were all in the same world — a world of hurt. Me, I was just A.C., the radioman, in that world. They counted on me because I had the ability to talk fast and get the whole squad out of trouble."

In the spring of 1970, back in the bush on patrol in a place called the Elephant Valley, Dave walked into the battle of his young life. "There were signs of a major force movement," he recalls.

Worn-out paths, trampled bushes." At the river path crossing, the 8-man unit split up and set up an ambush. As the Marines crouched in the bushes, a large North Vietnamese Army force appeared on the opposite riverbank and began wading across the river. "The lieutenant whispers, 'don't fire until I give the word". When the NVA walked up the bank, the Marines opened fire as one. "The first group takes part of the approaching column," explains Dave coolly. "We opened up on the back of the column. They never saw it coming. All they could do was run. It was a mess."

By Dave's calculations, the eight Marines dropped 16-25 of the enemy in the first burst of M-16 and M-60 fire. Dave himself accounted for three of the confirmed kills. "Once they made us there was no choice." Dave explains. "It was the first time I ever shot anyone."

As the North Vietnamese called in reinforcements, the resulting firefight became frantic, loud and lethal. "It's not like the movies — you don't hear the "zing" going by your ear — it's more like a loud "pow,"" Dave says. "Because we were outnumbered, I ask for a fast extraction "I called in, 'we're in serious trouble, we need a ladder extraction.' I'm screaming, 'get us out of here.'"

The Chinook swooped in at Dave's bidding. With the enemy closing in, the jungle crackling with automatic gunfire, the only feasible escape was a dangerous maneuver called a ladder extraction. The Chinook hovered above the patrol, who continued firing at the oncoming enemy. A nylon ladder was lowered from the CH-46. In any ladder extraction, the last two men to grab on to the dangling nylon lifeline and lift off from the ground are the radioman and "the boss, the LT."

As the NVA closed in, young Lance Corporal Dave Sikes thought maybe his luck and his faith in a promising future back in America's heartland were about to end. The ponderous Chinook hovered above his head, twin rotors pumping hot jungle air down upon his head. The sleek circling Cobras drew NVA fire and spit machine gun rounds in low staccato burps. At the last possible moment, with the ride home literally rising out of reach, the stocky Marine made a final lunge amid the deafening cacophony of gunfire. His grip held. "We were very fortunate," says Dave with a slow shake of his head.

The Chopper lifted off fast as Dave and his comrades hung on for the ride of their lives. Swinging in the breeze, all eight made it safely back to Da Nang.

After that, the squad had earned a couple of days of easy duty and an occasional warm beer at the local hutch of a bar. Life back at headquarters camp in Da Nang is a kind of welcome tedium.

Judy wrote every day, but the Marines meter out the distribution. Dave received them five at a time. She wrote about the minutia of everyday life, and Dave cherished every detail. Kerri was growing up, learning to walk — "she'd tell me everything that happened that day," Dave recalls.

Routinely, the tedium and desperation of camp life was interrupted by the jolting reality of death. One of Dave's best friends was killed in an ambush. "He took four or five of the enemy with him," Dave recalls. Amazingly, none of Dave's patrol mates had been hurt. "We were just lucky," he says unable to conceal a hint of guilt. "When you eat, sleep, shower and go to the bathroom with a group of guys, in a way you're closer than family. I was happy that none of the guys in my patrol had been hit. But every week at church they memorialized another Marine in our division who wasn't coming home."

Back on patrol, each new excursion into the bush was an unwritten mystery. When would their luck go south? A couple of patrols without drawing fire was followed by another life-changing close death encounter.

As summer burned on, and the end of his tour came slowly into sight, Dave experienced the same range of attitudes that most Vietnam veterans recognize. "When you first get in-country, you're scared to death," he explains. "In the middle of your tour, you just don't care anymore, because there's no way out. When you get short, you're scared to death again, and you don't want to go on patrol. You know that you're pressing your luck every time out."

Lance Corporal Dave Sikes was now a card-carrying member of "Charlie's Hunting Club," with confirmed kills and more near-death experiences than he cares to remember to this day. After an engagement, the 1st Reconn Battalion sometimes left one of these calling cards behind — inscribed with "we deal in death" — for the enemy to find and fear. Thirty years later, Dave still carries the card in his wallet.

But in the steaming late summer of 1970, in the jungles of Vietnam, Dave officially passed over the invisible demarcation line into the category of short-timer. "As a short-timer you didn't want to suit up. You were very careful. On patrol you walk slowly, with your face down, to see what you might step on."

As the days lengthened and Dave's attitude got "short" in military parlance, it wasn't a booby trap or an enemy round that finally put the young Marine on his back. It was a disease injected into his body by a tiny mosquito. "I got malaria in August," he says. "They transferred me to a medical ship in the South China Sea."

Lost in fever and restless dreams a Navy nurse entered his room aboard the USS Sanctuary. The doctors are mainly tied up with more serious cases — amputated limbs and brain wounds that will leave their victims dead or diminished for life. "Happy birthday Corporal," she says smiling. "How old are you?" "I'm 21," Dave responds without enthusiasm.

"I was 21 years old — legal at last. Instead of spending my birthday having a drink with Judy or my buddies in a bar, I was getting my fluids from an intravenous bag floating on a hospital ship with a 104-degree temperature."

Gradually the medicine took hold and Dave recovered his strength. The real milk and potatoes he got to eat on the medical ship helped. In a few weeks, he was transported back to camp in Da Nang. One warm September day he is hailed down by a sergeant who asks matter-of-factly, "We got your orders to go home. Can you ship out tomorrow?"

Dave sat quietly in the seat of the airliner staring out the porthole at the puffy clouds and green and tan patchwork of farmland below — such a different view from the jungle canopy he had peered into so many times prior to another insertion, another patrol into the unknown. He realized his return home is another kind of journey into uncertainty. "I was petrified when I walked off the plane — I was back in a different world from the one I left in Vietnam, and even the one I left when I shipped out to Nam a year before."

The whole family was at the airport to greet him. Dave hugged Judy and Kerri fiercely, trying hard to make up for lost time he knew he could never recover. Judy had stayed up all night. She was nervous and anxious. Now, both of Dave's girls were crying in his arms. "I felt like I had been released from solitary confinement after a year," he recalls. "Kerri had grown up so much."

Dave had a lot to get used to: a soft bed, good food, the fall chill in the southern Illinois air. He had to remind himself occasionally to watch the colorful language he had learned in the Corps. He struggled to comprehend the hostility he saw on television directed toward the military, toward the war that he had been proud to fight. Walking around the neighborhood, having lunch in his favorite Belleville spots, he was greeted warmly. "Semper Fi," an old friend says, patting Dave on his broad back. There was still pride here in the heartland of America. But on the evening news Walter Cronkite showed scenes of students back east burning draft cards and storming administration buildings. The clothes, the hair, the music all spoke to a strange new world that left him unsettled — feeling not quite at home in his new surroundings.

In February 1971, he was discharged from the Marine Corps. The Sikes family returned to their home on 17th Street in Belleville, where Dave was delighted to spend hours playing with Kerri, making houses out of old sea ration boxes. To scratch his adventurous itch, he raced motorcycles. But the energetic young man, who was quickly maturing into his role as father and family man, had no regrets about leaving the Marine Corps. "I was grateful to the Corps for turning me into a man," Dave says. "I went to Vietnam and I came back alive, and many guys I knew weren't nearly that lucky. I had defied death for so long that I felt like a cat with nine lives. The problem was, I didn't quite know how many I had left."

In the years ahead, as Dave s' family grew and his life with Judy become even fuller, his thoughts of Vietnam and the cold touch of death receded into the background, but never entirely left. He knew that his family was blessed, that they honored the Lord in their home and in their hearts. But deep in his soul he understood that no measure of goodness, faith or preparation could deflect death's reach when the time of reckoning was at hand.

For the Sikes family — happy, vital, at home and at peace in their small-town American lives — that time and test were looming.

E.J., Clara and Dave (18 mos Old)

Homecoming

The frightened teenager takes a final, quizzical look into her new baby boy's brown eyes. She hesitates for a long second, pats the receiving blanket where his tiny backside warms the cloth and gives it shape. In that instant, she says a silent prayer that he will be safe, a good boy all his life. She thinks, "If the Lord wills, maybe we'll see one another again some day," but with her not yet a woman's intuition, she knows that's not likely. With a sigh and a resigned nod she hands her child over to a nun who has spoken kindly to her during her two-week hospital stay. The sister returns the nod and cradles the baby to her chest. The girl's eyes are full of tears. The baby seems to smile at his young mother, a child herself. She nods again. She mouths the words good-bye, but there is no sound. Without speaking, the nun turns quickly on her heels and leaves the room with her tiny package. The girl is alone, more alone than she has ever felt.

The 15-year-old had come to southern Illinois, to St. Mary's Hospital in East St. Louis, Illinois, from Chicago to have her out-of-wedlock baby. Her middle-class parents were embarrassed when they discovered their daughter's unmentionable secret. They made arrangements early on in the unwanted pregnancy to send the girl away from prying friends and anguished family members. They had relatives downstate. East St. Louis is a good 300 miles south — a world away, then and now.

The city of East St. Louis — in those days a smaller version of Carl Sandberg's Chicago, "hog butcher for the world" — was, nevertheless, a thriving, mostly white, largely prosperous blue collar haven in 1949 across the river from larger St. Louis. Goods and freight flowed down the railroad tracks from the north for transfer in East St. Louis to Mississippi River barges and points east and west. Corn and coal were loaded back on the train cars at the East St. Louis railway stations to feed and fuel the bellies and furnaces of folks around the nation.

It's a region historically populated by hard-working, salt-of-the-earth citizens with aspirations and lifestyles as solid as the fertile ground that spreads out flat and endless from the banks of the nearby Mississippi. Today, East St. Louis has descended into blight, trapped in the grip of white flight and urban decay, but the neighboring Illinois communities — towns like Belleville, Millstadt and Murphysborough — retain their Germanic work ethic and no-nonsense charm.

The little brown-eyed infant, quiet now in the nun's black-robed arms, was one Chicago export destined to remain in southwestern Illinois for the rest of his life. The only remnant of his absent mother's hometown, which he carried into his future, were the "big shoulders" Sandberg made famous in his poem — a broad foundation that one day would balance the 165-pound kegs he unloaded from his beer truck.

The little orphan led a happy, if unaware existence for five months at St. Mary's, a handsome six-story structure standing only a few miles from the riverfront. The nurses, nuns and even an occasional doctor took good care of the baby, even though they were frequently preoccupied with their routine duties. Despite spending a good deal of time amusing himself in his crib, and the cruel reality that he remained nameless and parentless, the person that would become Dave Sikes was undeniably healthy and growing by the day.

In the nearby Illinois town of Belleville, the county seat of this piece of southwestern Illinois, just 20 miles due east of St. Louis, Clara and EJ Sikes yearned for a baby to love. Clara couldn't have children. Her twin pillars of support through the grief that engulfed her after learning that she was barren, were her husband, EJ, and the Catholic Church. With the always-reliable EJ, a sergeant in the newly created U.S. Air Force, unable to help her fulfill her obsession to become a mother, Clara turned to the church and Catholic Charities. The Sikes would seek to adopt a baby.

In 1949, the adoption was a streamlined undertaking compared with the grueling bureaucratic obstacle course that parents endure nowadays. Still, the Sikes filled out detailed paperwork to establish their suitability for parenthood in the eyes of the state and of the church. Over several months of waiting, Clara got to know the earnest young priest who coordinated the local Catholic Charities organization. The depth of Clara's longing for a child touched Father Reeb deeply. He would become a lifelong family friend who would lend his spiritual support at other times of pain and need.

In early 1950 he called Clara at home with news of a motherless child who had been at St. Mary's for five months. Clara trusted Father Reeb's judgment. "This baby is meant for us," she told EJ. The paper work was drafted before Clara and EJ ever saw the boy they would name David.

EJ, though apprehensive about the changes a child would bring to their lives, wanted his wife to be happy and whole. The baby's caretakers at St. Mary' even agreed to bring the 5-month-old to the Sikes' home.

On a cold, crisp February day in 1950, Clara and EJ waited nervously in the small parlor of their rented Belleville home waiting for their son to arrive. EJ placed his big right hand over Clara's small, white-gloved left hand. She stared ahead into the future saying nothing. Finally, she broke through the thickening tension. "They say he is fat and healthy."

"That's good," E.J smiled and nodded. He knew his wife wasn't looking for a response.

A black sedan pulled up in front of the house. Bright red crosses had been painted on the car's side panels. Clara heard the gravel crunching under the tires. EJ let the curtains fall back to cover the picture window, from where he had been standing vigil. "A priest and two sisters," he alerted Clara. E.J, who had been raised Baptist, but went out of his way to respect his wife's devoutly Catholic practices, had always been amused by the nuns in their black smocks and white trim. "Penguin," he had referred to one once, only to receive a look back from Clara that the Louisiana native recognized immediately as a short sample of something uncomfortably close to eternal damnation.

The Sikes met the St. Mary's delegation at the front door. They all shook hands, but Clara's gaze was pulled to a small white shape floating amid a beaming nun's black habit. The smiling sister was holding the most beautiful baby that Clara had ever seen. "He *isssss* fat," Clara cooed. She meant that he was the definition of baby health, with a robust appetite that would fortify him against winter ills and the lifelong dangers of the world. The baby's chubby cheeks were pink, his eyes large, brown and piercing. "He is perfect," she began to cry, and EJ wasn't about to disagree. He held his son for the first time and knew instinctively that Clara had been right all along. The boy would make them whole. EJ would teach his son about airplanes and engines and baseball. Yes, Clara was right as usual. The boy would give new purpose to their lives.

Their first responsibility as new parents was to clothe their son. Catholic Charities and St. Mary's Hospital couldn't afford to give away perfectly good garments along with babies. At least that was their line. Clara was delighted to exchange the tattered blue jumper her new son was wearing for a sharp red suit with matching cap and knickers. As she changed the round, gurgling infant, she realized they were smiling at each other in a way that Clara recognized instinctively. She knew it meant more than a random exploding gas bubble in her baby's belly. To Clara, their shared joy was the unbounded happiness of two lost souls who had finally found each other. Even then, in 1950, at 5 months, as he kicked and thrust his uncoordinated arms toward the shape above him in his new crib in his new room, the newest member of the Sikes family was glad finally to be home.

Clara named the baby David, because, like King David, her little one had overcome oversized obstacles to arrive safely in her arms. Her pride in his girth and eating prowess never wavered. She giggled in delight as David wolfed down the cereal and peaches she spooned into his churning mouth. The fair-haired bruiser weighed 19 pounds at five months.

Years later, when EJ had passed, and Clara was holding court around the pinochle table, she would recall to her lady friends that "David was a good baby — he wasn't used to all the attention we gave him when we got him home." And then she would look skyward, tug at her eye glasses, and flashing the same smile that lit up her face on that

February day when they brought her son home to her, declare with infallible knowledge, "God gave me this baby."

Clara never talked about David's real mother. She didn't know and didn't want to know, he would later observe. His parents told him about the circumstances of his birth when David was in junior high. The news had surprisingly little impact then. The young boy's life was untroubled and satisfying. He yearned strongly for little more than the usual romantic fantasies that capture a teenage boy's daydreams. Only later, as an adult Dave faced the most threatening health challenges of his life, would he look for clues to his condition in his mysterious heritage. When he was denied access to his birth records, Dave quickly gave up the search.

Partly he gave up that futile investigation because of his love and respect for the only mother he had ever known. Dave's adoptive mother Clara was born in 1921, the oldest of five children. She was delivered, as was the custom in those days, at her father's home in Smithton, Illinois, 10 miles down the road from Belleville. She had bright blue eyes and dark hair that turned snow white in her later years. Clara was tiny in stature — only 5-foot even — but driven by an unconquerable spirit, a big sense of humor and a love of laughter.

The former Clara Berkel was fiercely devoted to her husband, EJ, a southern gentleman with a natural deference to women. "He put women on a pedestal made of gold," says Dave of his father's self-depreciating charm. Clara, for her part, never exploited her husband's mild manner, choosing, for example, to stay at home and take care of David, and later, David's sister, instead of pursuing a career.

Neither did she press him to conform his religious beliefs to her fiercely held Catholicism. His was a personal brand of faith, but a confident give-and-take that included frequent personal conversations with the Lord. That was good enough, she thought for EJ, but not, by any means, for David, whom she insisted go to mass regularly, like his mother, and attend Catholic schools.

David inherited his adventurous streak — his willingness, as a young man, to try everything from motorcycle racing to volunteering for one of the military's most dangerous outfits — from Clara. She worked with him tirelessly as a child. When he would fail at a game or a task she would make him try again until he got it right. Her lessons and expectation were stern, but always tempered with a winning smile, an infectious laugh. It was the same laugh that Dave would one day recognize in his daughter Kerri.

But in the 1950s and 1960s, as Dave's body grew broad and strong — though, like Clara, never tall — she pushed him hard. While the first American military advisors invaded Vietnam; while the Beatles invaded America on The Ed Sullivan Show; while JFK challenged the nation's citizens to give back to society beyond their own self interests; while Martin Luther King Jr. marched in American towns far away from Belleville, Illinois, Clara focused on turning her boy into a man. EJ instructed him in sports — even coached David in little league football and baseball. But it was Clara's voice from the bleachers that penetrated the crowd noise and drove him forward on the ball field. She challenged her son, who preferred working with his hands and body over academics, to make good grades. When Dave became interested in girls, Clara was tough on his dates, although she would eventually come to love his young wife, Judy, as a daughter. When Dave left home for good, she continued to talk to her son almost every day.

Though less demanding than Clara, more willing to let life unfold as it will, Dave's father also molded Dave's personality with a gentle hand that put the premium on honor, duty, quiet dignity and respect for the rights of others, especially those in need.

EJ was proud of his southern heritage, and carried those values with him throughout his life and around the world. Born in Monroe, Louisiana, in 1917, EJ had 13 brothers and sisters. As a youngster he sweated and scratched his hands raw picking cotton in the steaming Louisiana fields.

One of EJ's first assignments in the Army Air Corps was a tour at Scott Air Field near Belleville, Illinois, just across the Mississippi from St. Louis. Southern Illinois seemed a world away for a country boy from Louisiana who missed his family with a passion. But EJ, a handsome young man with a quiet confidence, met new people easily. He was a big man, 6 foot 2, over 200 pounds. A friend of a friend soon set the southerner up on a date with a petite brunette nurse's aide named Clara Berkel who worked at St. Elizabeth's Hospital in downtown Belleville. The seemingly mismatched couple — the tall, slow-talking southern Protestant and the little, vivacious, devoutly Catholic Midwesterner — hit it off at the level that always transcends background. They fell in love. But love, in 1942, fell second to the requirements of a world at war. Days after their marriage at a Catholic church in

Belleville, young EJ was flown to the Aleutian Islands for a three-year hitch to guard America's back door against the Japanese.

When he finally returned to Clara from that remote part of the world that had been his island home for the entire war, the solid Midwestern earth of his wife's homeland seemed like a great place to raise a family.

EJ appreciated the value of family and children. When David came along, he showered a great deal of affection on his young son. But it was the affection and respect that the big man showed David's mom that impressed and permanently influenced the youngster. "I always got a lot of reassurance and happiness from the way he would gently hug my mother," remembers Dave. "It was kind of funny because of the difference in their sizes." EJ demonstrated his respect for his wife in many ways — watching his language, and warning his young son to always do the same. He himself would sometimes slip around David, allowing one of those colorful epithets the military had taught him to surface at a stressful moment. But David knew his father's anger was always fleeting — never held in his big heart. EJ punished him only reluctantly and rarely raised a hand to the boy. He treated his son, as he treated the rest of the world, with considered respect.

When David was 6-years-old, his father was transferred to West Germany. While in Germany, Clara made the decision to adopt again. The Sikes' adopted a German infant and named her Jean Marie. Jean Marie's mother was from a small town called Meinz. Like David's real mother, she made the tortured choice to give her daughter up to a family who could do more for her.

David and Jean bonded quickly. The boy hadn't yet learned the story of his own adoption, but he sensed a deep, nameless need inside his new baby sister's eyes that reminded him of something real and familiar. Despite the sudden change in his status as his parents' only child and constant source of pride, David wasn't jealous. He played contentedly and without being asked with his sister. He told her about their real home across the ocean in a place called America.

Upon returning to Illinois, life for Dave, Jean, Clara and EJ was full, woven lovingly together by family and extended family threads of tradition. Dave's grandparents and uncles and aunts were always around to share a memory, a laugh and a story. The house was alive with the smells of cooking, the chatter of his mother and aunts as they canned fruits and vegetables, the shriek of “Gin” as one of those women in his life won at Rummy. Or maybe it was a team match of Euchre or Pinochle. In any case the white smoke of cigarettes and the foam of newly poured beer blended together to cloud the scene. The men in the Berkel and Sikes families, like many Belleville German clans, were big beer-drinkers.

The celebrations gained sharp contrast from a constant, focused background of hard work, reliability and clear commitment to family, country and community. As a little boy David helped EJ in the yard, but growing up, the broad-shouldered boy held down a summer job at the local market, where he lifted sacks of produce with ease and followed directions willingly and carefully. That same attention to detail came harder for David in school, but he discovered early on that he had inherited his dad’s mechanical aptitude

When Dave finished grade school, there was never a doubt that he would attend Cathedral, the Belleville Diocese only all-boys Catholic high school. David played baseball at the sports-minded school. He enjoyed the sense of camaraderie the boys gained from their status apart from the public school system, in spite of the ribbing they sometimes took from the public boys about the “unnatural” decision to endure life without girls.

That was an unenlightened opinion though — one that any Cathedral boy could quickly repudiate. There were girls, the girls from Notre Dame, the all-girl's Catholic high school, which provided the cheerleaders for Cathedral's teams, and the nervous attendees for the school's numerous mixers. Dave went to the mixers alright, but didn't much like to dance. In fact, he found it more than a little intimidating to even approach any of the perfumed, bouffanted females that lingered in the darkness by the gym bleachers at those events.

Dave couldn't have known that the only girl he would ever love was attending Belleville's public high school, Belleville Township, at the same time that he was earning his varsity letter at Cathedral.

Judy Reynolds was born Aug. 18 1949, just six days before her future husband. Her parents, Lester and Helen of Murphysborough, Ill., moved to Belleville in the early 1950's. In those days, Lester, Helen, little blond-haired Judy and her three older sisters lived in a rented frame house on South High Street in Belleville, just eight blocks away from the service station where Judy's Dad dutifully toiled every day of the week, except Sundays.

Lester and Helen Reynolds, who struggled to put food on the table for their family, were more than satisfied with three daughters. In fact Lester had sought out the relatively rare option in 1948 of a vasectomy to ensure that outcome. When Helen was told, six months after the procedure, she was pregnant again, she cried. "It wasn't that she had any doubts about dad — vasectomies in those days weren't such a sure thing — it was simply the burden of knowing they couldn't afford another child," explains Judy with a nod of understanding. "My mother and father loved me despite the hardships".

In 1967 an awakening of a romantic kind was looming on the horizon when high school senior Judy Reynold's fate finally collided head-on with the destiny of a young man with whom she was already vaguely aware of, but had never given a passing thought. Yet they had grown up at times living within a few blocks of each other.

Judy's friend, Debbie Maddox, was arranging a double date. "Come on Judy, it'll be fun" Debbie said. "Mike and I will be there. What could it hurt?" Judy knew this was a losing battle. You didn't say 'no' easily to Debbie, but this was a bad idea — a double date with someone she had never spoken to in her life, David Sikes, the

Cathedral boy with the greased-back DA haircut.

Judy's dating experience was limited to a few other forgettable occasions when the overeager boys had made their dating objectives all too clear for Judy's taste. "I hadn't been on many dates and I wasn't comfortable with the idea," she admits. Her small world and cautious approach to love was about to change — a little. "OK, I'll go just so you have someone to go with, but I won't promise to be nice to him if he's a jerk, and if you two leave us alone, I'll kill you both."

Their first date was a disaster. Judy being shy and unsure of this guy she hardly knew and for Dave, unskilled himself in the strategies of dating and understanding women, thought that Judy had to be a girl with all the boyfriends she could want. But today he says quietly, with a sense of irony, "I guess we were just nervous. We didn't really talk because we didn't know what to talk about. I really believed she was a socialite, a bit stuck up, and if we hadn't given it one more try, I would have made the biggest mistake of my life.

That second, salvage attempt didn't take place for four months. In May, Belleville Township High hosted a school dance back at Panorama, and Judy nodded her head when Dave approached her sheepishly, asking her to dance. As they moved as one in the darkness beneath the silver ball reflecting light in supernova spirals around the room, they held their silence, and each other. But something had changed unalterably between them. Something in Dave's touch told Judy that this was a special guy and the way Judy followed him told Dave that they might have something together after all.

After the dance, Judy's family hosted a Memorial Weekend barbecue to honor the graduating seniors. Judy asked Mike Heafner to extend an invitation to Dave. After dinner, Dave took Judy for a ride. This time, the nervousness was a distant memory. When there was silence, it was comfortable, the kind of confidence that exists between people in love when there's no need to fill up every moment with words. It was the sudden realization that a glance, an unsaid understanding was the most perfect communication possible.

"I enjoyed just riding around in Dave's car listening to music, and it hit me how nice he was — the opposite of my first impression," Judy explains. "I had been with a number of guys who were after one thing. Dave was always a gentleman — a real genuine guy. I started noticing things about him that didn't come out in normal conversation — his gentleness, kindness, but also the pride he took in himself and everything he did.

Dave was equally overwhelmed by the feelings that were flooding in for the first time. '"I started thinking this could work," he recalls. "Now I was calm with her, more comfortable. I spent some time with her parents, and they seemed to accept me."

Their first kiss came during an outing to a man-made lake in Granite City, Ill. They swam all day, bought hot dogs and French Fries at the concession stand and danced under the moonlight to a four-piece band that assembled every Friday and Saturday night at 8. Dave wanted to kiss her while they danced, but he held back, understanding that a public setting, no matter how intimate, wouldn't do. They both held back the feeling that had been building steadily, powerfully. He drove her back to Belleville, to her sister's house where she was babysitting for her nieces and nephews.

In the front hallway, as he said goodbye, Dave embraced the only woman he would ever love. He held Judy very close to him, closer than ever before. Then, he kissed her firmly and gently as the kids slept in another room and the world turned slowly, unnoticed beneath their feet. They sensed nothing else in the Universe except the beating of their hearts and the softness of each other's touch. From that point on, their lives together would point in one direction through the brightest imaginable and darkest endurable moments.

The seeds of sorrow

Kerri's body lay in the open oaken casket her mother had insisted upon despite the damage to her oldest daughter's broken body. She was no more alive, like the real Kerri, than the lifeless form Dave, Judy and Krista had identified on the metal gurney at St. Elizabeth's Hospital two nights earlier. News about the crash and Kerri's death had spread quickly through the small, insular community of Millstadt. That morning a story in the *Belleville New-Democrat* was illustrated by a photograph of her crumpled Geo Tracker and a description of the accident scene quoting the investigating officer. An obituary in another section of the paper had announced the time and location for her visitation, funeral mass and burial.

The news of Kerri's death, though, spread more rapidly than the delivery of Belleville's only daily. Her lifetime of active involvement in school and community life, the warmth of her personality and the magnetism of her smile ensured that her devastating death notice pulsed instantaneously through the veins and arteries of local community awareness.

It wasn't as though death and tragedy were

an unheard of occurrence in a rural town like Millstadt, but the relative rarity of crime, accidents or natural deadly disasters leant special significance to the loss of any community member — especially a child of the community. That is the enduring gift of small-town life all over the world, and the small towns and villages of the American Midwest offer as genuine an example of this precious natural resource as anywhere else. In the heartland of America, as in other connected places in this world, people depend on each other and on each other's word. The triumph or failure — the good fortune or bad luck — of any citizen is meaningful for your neighbor. The viability of a mom and pop store, the ascension of a high school or college graduate, the 50th wedding anniversary of an honored couple — every accomplishment and every misdeed, every honored commitment and every lack of faith — has an impact.

The Sikes were just one strong thread in that close-knit fabric of Millstadt, Illinois. Sturdy Dave Sikes — a familiar formidable figure, driving his beer truck, calling on his customers around the region, extending a thousand firm hand shakes. Busy Judy, carrying out her duties on the St. James Catholic School's athletic booster committee. And Kerri and Krista, stopping at the local candy store on the way home from school to buy some licorice, paying for their treat with a few nickels and two heart-felt smiles. These were the gestures and the memories and the sense of shared loss that drove a large part of the community of Millstadt to Strauss Funeral Home on that cold, windy afternoon on Jan. 25, 1991.

As the crowd began to line up outside the funeral home, family members and close friends inside paid their last respects to Kerri Sikes. Those who approached the coffin and knelt or stood at Kerri's side didn't know that some bones in her fragile, pretty face had been fractured. But the funeral home director was expert in his craft and had managed, through shadings of color, to restore an appearance of vibrancy and delicacy to Kerri's cold cheeks. The flecks of blood had been scrubbed away. "I needed one more day to say goodbye. I kissed her one more time," Judy recalls.

The immediate family was alone with Kerri's body near the casket. Dave's mother arrived and embraced Dave, Judy and Krista. Everyone was crying. Father Gene Neff, a close family friend, who had baptized Kerri and Krista was also on hand, but despite his training, found himself at a loss for words in the face of such tragedy.

Intermittently, family members gazed over at her body — motionless, eyes closed — and then down again at the flowers, and color photographs of the brightly smiling Kerri in her cheerleader uniform, in her graduation gown. The images couldn't be reconciled. The girl in the picture reflected unbounded energy — her life force seems to jump at them, momentarily jolting them awake from their numb, anesthetized thoughts. Kerri was dressed in dark pants and a favorite olive green sweater that her mother knew she would have liked. She always dressed modestly, even at public occasions like this. Hours for the visitation were 4-9 p.m. The sun was setting rapidly and a steady stream of friends, teachers, classmates, co-workers and family acquaintances moved by quietly. In hushed tones they expressed their condolences to Judy and Dave who stood in the middle aisle of the funeral home's largest visitation room. An invisible hand seemed to prop them up. Only when the mother of one of Dave and Judy's friends approached her — a woman Judy remembered who had lost her own grown son two years before — did the light of recognition turn on in Judy's bloodshot eyes. Without words the two mothers clung to each other.

Judy recognized another woman who was

Kerri's boss at the Stan Gellman Design firm. The woman passed a card to Judy that read:
"Kerri… I loved her laugh. She could make me laugh and I wouldn't even know what was so funny. She was so generous and willing to do anything at all for you. She truly was a unique and high-spirited individual. I will miss her very much."

The next morning St. James Church in Millstadt was again filled for the funeral mass. The priest commended Kerri's soul to God. He said that Kerri was in a better place. The hardest challenge is for those left behind, he added, he asked God to grant the Sikes the grace and strength to carry on in faith and hope for the day when we all be reunited with the Lord in heaven.

That prayer, vague, only half remembered, hovered in Judy's consciousness later that day as she witnessed the first handfuls of dirt tossed down upon her daughter's coffin. The dark earth mixed in with a few random snowflakes that began floating down from the dark January sky. There on that cold, hard ground at the foot of her daughter's grave and later at the West End Tavern where the family gathered for lunch, a quiet shell-shocked Judy contemplated how they would ever survive this blow. How could a God they had believed was on their side let this unspeakable thing happen

Today, Dave and Judy admit that their initial reaction was anger — anger at God, anger at everything that had seemed safe and familiar and trustworthy. Everything had turned upside down. Nothing was as it appeared on the surface, and even the normal relationships of life began to break down. Their anger separated them from the community that had always functioned as a foundation source of strength and comfort. "When Kerri died our "compassionate friends" would say, 'Someday, you'll feel better.' But we kept asking ourselves, 'How could we ever feel normal again. A week later, a friend of the Sikes put their challenge in simple words. "It's a journey that you can't go around or under — you have to go through it."

The Sikes noticed that even some of their closest friends and family members were overwhelmed by Kerri's loss and the torrent of emotion swirling around Judy, Dave and Krista. "Many people kind of backed off for a year — I guess because they just didn't know what to say," Dave says with a resigned shrug. "Even our own family had trouble finding the right words. I guess it was understandable."

Dave tried to go forward in his customary

no-nonsense manner. As he carried out his daily duties driving his truck for Fritz Distributors, he dealt as well as he could with the unwelcome reminders of Kerri's death. "I didn't want to face anybody," he recalls. "People were always asking me, 'How are you doing?' Sometimes, they hadn't even heard about Kerri's accident, so they'd ask, 'How's your family?' I'd think to myself, 'I can't take this.' I knew they were just trying to be nice, but I really couldn't even bear to mention Kerri or the accident."

For Judy, the tears flowed freely often: "I remember crying in public situations in front of all kinds of people," she says today, even managing a slight smile at the pain and embarrassment of the bitter memory. Judy was employed as a secretary at a St. Louis bank at the time. She had returned about a month after Kerri's death, but after a short period of trying to battle through her despair, the always hard-working grieving mother had to stop. "I wasn't doing myself or them any good," she explains. "Everything was different for me. I would go into the bathroom, lock myself into a stall and cry." Initial counseling sessions, arranged by the bank, offered the faintest beginnings of self-awareness. In a family where hectic activities built around family, friends and cherished traditions pushed the pace of life dizzyingly ahead, life slowed to a crawl.

Spring flowed haltingly into summer and Krista's high school graduation created another bittersweet emotional flash point for Dave and Judy. Their surviving daughter, blonde and blue eyed as Kerri had been, stood up at the reverberating call of her name through a microphone. She adjusted her maroon graduation cap and moved confidently, happily, up the steps to accept her diploma. Her parents, in metal folding chairs on the same Belleville West football field where Kerri had graduated four years before, struggled to reconcile their warring emotions. At times, blinking back their tears, they were uncertain if the figure rising to the platform and the principal's outstretched hand was really Krista, or if somehow time had not just slowed down, but reversed itself. Could that be Kerri's wide smile lighting up the stage, could it be her delicate hand grasping the paper that signified her passage into adulthood, into a new life. No, an abrupt scratch in the PA system brought them back to June 1991 and the ongoing struggle to find meaning in their cruelly altered existence.

After the graduation ceremony, Dave and Judy struggled to find peace with another decision.

Krista asked if she could go out with some friends to celebrate their accomplishments. The Sikes had never been overbearing parents, but every instinct cried out to them to protect their last remaining child with every power left in their reserves. Krista was all they had left. She represented the full measure of their remaining focus as a family and the living treasure of a lifetime of parental commitment. "In the end, we decided to let her go out," says Judy, a lone tear welled up at the corner of eye. "We knew we couldn't protect her forever. We only asked her to call us and let us know where she was.

In November 1991, Dave reached quickly to his backhand to smash his return of a serve from his racquetball partner, a Millstadt buddy. Dave's thick powerful forearms are tailor-made for racquetball and the athletic man loved the competitive advantage that years of lifting beer kegs had given him. Racquetball courts and golf courses had replaced motorcycle tracks for the former combat Marine, who had lived life on the edge in earlier years. "I raced motorcycles in Belleville and White City," Dave says. "But my specialty was hill climbing." Dave gave up racing when he saw a good friend die on the track, but he hung on to his 305 Honda until 1987.

As he competed in a semi-friendly game of racquetball with a buddy in the fall of 1991, Dave still enjoyed coming out on top. But something was wrong this time. His return is perfectly placed, but instead of moving quickly into position for the kill shot, Dave has stopped in the middle of the court. He was doubled over at the waist. Rolling spasms of coughing wracked his body. "I had played racquetball for 15 years on weeknights, in leagues, and that was the first time I ever stopped in the middle of a game. I remember my partner saying, 'what's the deal?' Coughing like that was unusual for me, but I wasn't worried, even though I was having some pain in my chest along with the coughing. I couldn't tell my buddy what the deal is. I was 41, and I thought the pain was just part of getting older."

Despite his vague sense of unease about the episode, Dave didn't go to the doctor. Like many men of his generation and background, seeing a physician was the option of last resort. Dave had had a handful of checkups over the years. Still, his overall solid health and good fortune, despite the malaria he had contracted in Vietnam, and determination to generally swat away minor aches and occasional colds kept him away from the hospital or doctor's office.

He didn't tell the doctor about the coughing and he didn't share it with Judy. She was deeply engaged in her own struggle for survival. Krista had actually finished her high school classes in January, and spent the six-month period until her official graduation mostly home with her valiantly struggling mom. In the fall of 1991 Krista started junior college at Belleville Area College. "Her being home helped," recalls Judy. "When she was around I didn't let myself be overly sad. I think I found a certain amount of strength and control because I didn't want Krista to think I cared more about Kerri than her."

Using housework and staying busy as a kind of therapy, Judy describes her life at that time as a mission to simply stay sane. The Sikes had a pool built in the back yard that spring — a project and a pastime that Judy hoped would "bring us all together as a family."

But Judy knew that chores and swimming couldn't begin to heal the empty spot in her own heart and her family's spirit. The Sikes joined a support group for parents who have lost children. Judy found comfort in the stories and shared experiences of people who had known the devastation and darkness of losing the most precious thing in your life. “I thought it was a great help,” Judy says without hesitation. “But I was concerned that Dave didn’t seem to be getting more out of it. He just couldn’t open up.”

“I went because Judy wanted me to go,” admits Dave. “I just didn’t understand how rehashing everything — bringing all that pain up to the surface again — could do anybody any good.”

During the support group sessions — and at random unbidden moments — Judy would cry violently. The fair, delicate features of her face would swell up. Judy recalls that Dave would do his best to comfort her. He would hold her tightly to his broad chest, but he never cried. With a mighty exercise of his will, Dave would absorb the torment of his quaking partner as he pressed her closely to him, but not be stirred himself to tears. Today he admits quietly, tellingly that “I held it all in. I didn’t think crying would help.” Through their grief — acted out in polarized manners — one clear thought appeared riveted in their consciousness. Dave and Judy recall the words at the same time. “When would we have a normal life?”

For Judy, something short of normalcy would have been a welcome relief from the torment she was experiencing every breathing moment. Her daughters had meant the world to her, and the emptiness she was feeling seemed like a hole that was slowly growing and would soon swallow up her mind and her faith. "I was driving down the highway one day on my way home from work, and I knew instinctively that I had reached the end," she recalls. "I began screaming out loud at God, 'I can't stand it anymore! God, give me the strength to go on.' At that exact moment, I felt a sense of peace wash over me. All of a sudden, I realized that I had all the strength I needed. What I really needed was peace. He gave me what I didn't even know I needed, and even though I continued to grieve for Kerri, it was never again more than I could tolerate. I believe, with all my heart, that God will never give you more of a cross than you can bear. But you have to be willing to ask for help."

That theory would be sorely tested. On Christmas Eve, 1991, Dave — who had avoided doctors all his life — got so sick that he agreed to be driven to see a physician. He was burning up with a 102-degree temperature, throbbing aches and the full range of flu-like afflictions. A Belleville physician prescribed antibiotics. His symptoms hung on and by February 1992, he was in the hospital. Hospitalization for a man who had only missed three days of work in 20 years was nearly intolerable. But a festering doubt about his health was more troubling than even the coughing and the incapacitation. Dave was released from the hospital, but his breathing was becoming increasingly labored as his attending physician searched for the accurate diagnosis. The prediction was pneumonia, and a few days later, Dave was back in Memorial Hospital for a bronchosopy — in which a pulmonologist extracted tissue from Dave's lungs through his throat.

Based on those results and the realization of Dave's family practice physician that his patient's persistent symptoms needed specialized attention, Dave was referred to a pulmonary specialist. The dark-haired physician offered Judy and Dave a seat in his office after conducting his examination of Dave and reviewing his test results and X-rays. Judy hoped that a new physician with a fresh perspective might bring them a more positive diagnosis, but the slow-speaking physician's words now blotted out those hopeful thoughts. "Your husband has an influenza virus that is attacking his lungs," the doctor revealed in measured tones. "We will need him to be in the hospital for a couple of weeks to treat his condition."

With two weeks of hospital time ahead of him, Dave worried as much about missed work than his suddenly tenuous health. His fever went down after a week as the antibiotics flowed intravenously into his system. Dave's normally prodigious appetite faltered and the stocky man lost weight noticeably. Judy was back at work — this time at a Belleville bank — which made her nightly trips to Memorial Hospital a little closer. But the stress on her attitude and peace of mind was only growing. Seeing Dave visibly change before her eyes was more than alarming. Judy felt the first twinges of panic rising up in her own chest. She recalls thinking, "I just couldn't go through losing him on top of losing Kerri. We both thought Dave would start getting better any day now, but even after he got out of the hospital he really didn't improve. Whatever it was — and none of the doctors seemed to exactly put a finger on it — it simply wasn't going away."

Dave was out of the hospital after two weeks and back to work after a month and a half, despite his lack of improvement and uncertain diagnosis. Dave didn't like missing work, but the demands of his job couldn't be denied. Instead of easier duty, he was back on the same tough route, still working eight hours a day, unloading cases of beer and back-bending half barrels out of trucks with no air conditioning in the blistering Midwestern heat. He was having a heck of a time breathing. Because of his constant congestion, he was popping pain and sinus medicine at an alarming pace. Up to 16 pain pills a day and four of the sinus variety a day kept him going. His nose ran constantly. Dave was unaware that he was risking damaging his liver with the heavy ingestion of ibuprofen, but the impact of that possibility on his future lung transplant was nowhere on his radar screen. The bottom line was getting through another day.

Every six weeks the weakening Dave saw his pulmonologist. On each visit he got a new chest X-ray. In his doctor's modestly appointed office after every examination, he received the seemingly unalterable news that his lung capacity was decreasing. At one session, the doctor held up the actual X-ray and offered Dave an illustrated presentation that would have held a certain intellectual appeal to the mechanically inclined craftsman if the news wasn't pointing to his own steady physical decline.

"You started at 84 percent lung capacity," the doctor explained pointing to the somewhat murky-looking negative. You have gone steadily down from there to the point you can see in this image. In October 1992, the doctor presented a new X-ray to Dave and Judy sitting side-by-side on the couch in his office. "Your lungs are much worse," he says with finality. "There is nothing more I can do for you. You need a lung transplant"

A Candle in the Darkness

The doctor had said something about a transplant The words fell on the anxious couple — holding hands on the sofa — like an avalanche. It felt as though he had just sent Dave home to die. The weight of the words were crushing — echoing the words of another physician who, just a little more than a year earlier, had announced Kerri's death in the same emotionless cadence. "There is nothing more I can do."

Dave's pathology was perplexing, some kind of virus, non-identifiable, not treatable. The corrosive, malignant residue of Agent Orange exposure in Vietnam, perhaps? The doctor would fulfill his professional responsibility and point Dave in the only direction that could save his life — west toward the Washington University Medical Center and one of the nation's leading centers for treating lung disease.

Dave was referred to Dr. Robert Senior, a pulmonologist at the Jewish Hospital of St. Louis. Dave had never been to the Washington University Medical Center when he and Judy made the 40-minute drive from Millstadt to St. Louis' Central West End on a crisp October morning in 1992. He felt a little uneasy as he crossed the Poplar Street

Bridge over the Mississippi River.

As he steered left on the bridge, taking I64/US40 past the St. Louis Arch and Busch Stadium, he worried, not so much about how Dr. Senior would assess his chances to receive a transplant. He was more concerned about taking the right exit to get to Jewish Hospital. The whole idea of a transplant hovered outside the boundaries of his imagination. Dave had always been a practical man in terms of trusting what he could see and touch. He enjoyed learning about the mechanics of things — the inner workings of a HF radio set, a car engine. He had spent much less time thinking about theoretical, concepts that can't be measured. This much he knew — he was sick and getting sicker. Counting on some procedure that he didn't fully understand that was predicated on someone he didn't know giving him a new set of lungs was, from Dave's grounded perspective on that October morning, really not worth worrying about.

Dave liked Dr. Senior immediately because he seemed to embrace a similar no-nonsense approach to Dave's illness. He prescribed 100 milligrams of prednisone — a strong dose of the steroid-based drug designed to control Dave's smothering congestion and allow him to breathe easier. Beyond this important step, Dr. Senior finally put a name to the phantom affliction that had attacked Dave's body. "They call the disease IPF — Idiopathic Pulmonary Fibrosis — and they don't know what causes it," explains Dave. They do know that the body's own immune system won't attack it."

Dave got to know the route and environs of the Central West End and Washington University Medical Center very well over the next few months as he traveled there every two weeks to meet with Dr. Senior. He continued to work, but the prednisone was causing serious side-effects, at the heavier that usual dosage of 100 milligrams every day. Dave's hands shook and his vision blurred. As the proud man made his rounds every day, he would unload his half barrels and cases before meeting his customer — usually a long-known store proprietor — with an outstretched hand and an invoice. Squinting and struggling to point out the designated signature line, the pen sometimes falling from his shaking grasp, Dave would bend to the floor and fight back the nausea bubbling up in his gut. "How's that problem with your lungs," the old customer asked, concern apparent in his question. "Going great — no problem," Dave lied, determined to press ahead and make it to another stop. The usual feeling of well-being generated by steroids was quickly giving way to the pain of a deteriorating body, the dread of a threatened future and the frustration of a growing inability to fight back.

In December 1992, Dr. Senior decided a closer look at Dave's lungs was necessary. A lung biopsy was performed. After an incision was made through Dave's side, a device called a rib-spreader literally wedged and held his ribs apart, providing access to his shrinking lungs. An assessment of the diseased tissue by Dr. Senior reinforced the prediction that eventually a lung transplant would be necessary to save Dave's life. But before recommending Dave for the program, Dr. Senior wanted to continue to treat Dave with medication. The news wasn't unexpected, but an extremely sore Dave responded in the only way that made sense to him after a two-month convalescence. He tried to go back to work. "I was so sore I couldn't breathe," recalls Dave, noting the after-affects of the surgical procedure that had spread apart his ribs.

As Judy moved on to a new job as a secretary at Washington Park Continental Grain Company, Dave worked the night shift for Fritz Distributors. He loaded trucks with Miller beer and other brands by hand and operated a fork lift to stock pallets. With Dave gone evenings, and Krista busy with her classes at BAC and the typical nighttime activities of a fun-loving young woman, Judy was left many nights to her exhaustion and her troubled dreams. The constant projection of life without her partner pecked at her thoughts like a great foreboding black bird. "If I lose him, I won't be able to go on," she recalls thinking on those tortuous nights. As she turned her head restlessly to find the undiscoverable comforting side of her pillow, she reminded herself, "I've gone through this once and it has nearly killed me."

Still, there was no option for the battling Sikes but to take each day as it came. By June 1993, Dave's existence was reduced to fundamentals. "I just worked, took my drugs and slept," Dave says. Dave's medical costs were beginning to have an impact on the family's financial health as acutely as its physical and emotional well-being. With Dave at the end of his rapidly decreasing capacity and finally unable to continue working, Judy stepped into the breach. She got her insurance and securities licenses and started selling mutual funds and insurance. "But I wasn't very successful at it," she says. "I knew pretty quickly that I was not a salesman."

As a family, the Sikes relied on their kinetic lifestyles as an anecdote to the growing panic in their hearts. Judy would work all day at the grain company and then through the night making sales calls. "I was tired all the time," she says. Krista continued her classes at BAC part-time, while starting a new part-time job at Walmart's. A new ray of light, as well, was introduced into the darkening drama. Krista's boyfriend Randy — later her husband — was welcomed by Dave and Judy to the family. They found him to be a gentle soul who treated Krista with kindness and patience. His easy-going sense of humor and fun-loving nature filled a void for Krista, which had been empty since the loss of her mentor and sister Kerri. Dave, in particular enjoyed having another male's viewpoint around.

As the sweltering heat of a Midwestern summer gave way to the shorter days of fall, Dave was reduced to suffocating inactivity. "It was getting harder and harder to do anything," he recalls with a fresh wince. "At first, I sat around most of the day. It was extremely depressing, and to tell the truth, I thought they had just sent me home to die."

Dave's retrogressing lungs literally

underpowered him into a slow-motion hell. A simple shower was an ordeal, taking at least an hour. He seemed to be moving slower every day, straining to take in enough oxygen to fuel his lumbering motions. A typical day for Dave consisted of making himself a simple breakfast and watching TV. Judy would come home for lunch, but the conversations, for the first time in the whole course of Dave's illness, became strained. Judy was exhausted, doing her part to keep the family afloat financially, while Dave chaffed at his new situation. Both were frustrated by their inability to change what had happened to them. At a time when their love for one another had never been stronger, they were consumed with regret for the fate of their partner.

"We didn't really ever argue," Judy recalls. "Coming home to Dave was my only salvation, and he always supported me emotionally." Dave and Judy's relationship had changed perceptively since Kerri's death. They had the usual arguments that couples have. But after the death of their oldest daughter and Dave's sudden sickness, they held on to each other for balance and direction. "We were like two ships lost at sea," Judy says. "We were constantly searching for the shoreline and some ray of hope. The darkness, emptiness and helplessness we both felt couldn't be seen or felt by anyone else around us, so we clung to each other as though our lives depended on it — because they did."

A new direction appeared with Dave's first visit to Dr. Elbert Trulock, Barnes Hospital pulmonologist and a member of the lung transplant medical review team.

Drs. Senior and Trulock had come to a mutual decision — a lung transplant was among the dwindling treatment options that would have to be considered. But Dave learned at his first meeting with the soft-spoken Trulock that a large hurdle remained if he was to ultimately receive the transplant he desperately needed. As in the jungles of Vietnam, Dave was about to be tested severely, and his life depended on his passing that test.

The week-long evaluation of Dave ' fitness to receive a lung transplant began in November 1993 on Barnes Hospital's ninth floor. Psychiatric tests measured a variety of emotional stability issues in Dave's background — patience, perseverance, commitment to responsibility. A simple matter like Dave's ability to follow basic directions would be a life-saving factor in the eager patient's survival after the procedure he hoped for. Then, a dizzying array of medications and dosages would be necessary to combat Dave's immunity defenses if and when he received his new lungs. Beyond his emotional make-up the evaluation analyzed his physical suitability. Cardiologists used a catheter to test the flow of blood to his heart. Liver and infectious disease specialists discussed his medical history, including his Vietnam-era bout of malaria, and concluded that affliction wouldn't disqualify him. "I thought my Malaria would keep me off the list," Dave says. But I hung in and did whatever they told me. I was told that the selection committee would choose 10 out of 100 candidates, so I wasn't that optimistic, but this was my only shot."

Returning home after a week of grueling tests, Dave and Judy were struck by the helplessness of their situation. There was no additional case they could make to the interdisciplinary team of physicians and clinical experts that would advance their cause. Judy simmered inside, wanting to tell them more than she knew her man of few words would have communicated in his own behalf. If they knew about what it felt like to kiss the broken cheek bones of your oldest child before they closed the coffin door and took her away from your view for the rest of your life. If they knew what it was like to stand in her old bedroom, holding a favorite old stuffed bear growing wet from a cascade of tears. If they understood what if felt like to look across the kitchen table at Dave, with his oxygen canister on the seat where Kerri would have sat, and to imagine his place empty, as well. Did they realize whom else in the Sikes family they might be condemning if they failed to grant Dave his chance to go on holding them all together as he had always done? For Dave, the wait for an answer was equally stressful, but as was his custom, he had prepared himself for the worse. "I still looked at my situation as a death sentence," he explains. "I wasn't counting on the transplant, but Judy and I agreed that we needed to take some positive action to get us through the waiting."

They went to the library. At the Belleville Public Library they immersed themselves in information about transplants and lung disease. In a who's who volume of biographical information about local physician they even read about the latest doctor to tackle Dave's mysterious illness, Dr. Trulock. "We were excited by the article that indicated Dr. Trulock was one of the area's leading authorities on lung disease and that the lung transplant program at Barnes Hospital was considered one of the best in the nation" Judy says. "We learned that 70 percent of transplant patients survived the operation, but only 50 percent made it through the first year after their operation." Those odds don't sound great, but I could see Dave deteriorating in front of my eyes and, at the time, we took those statistics as hopeful numbers."

Rapid deterioration was equally evident to Dave's new physician, Dr. Elbert Trulock, who describes his patient's condition at that time in the cool, slightly Southern-accented tones of a clinician who has trained himself to maintain objectivity at all costs. "As is the case with most patients who come to see me, Dave had advanced pulmonary fibrosis. The referring physician, Dr. Senior, had made the diagnosis and was proceeding with standard medical treatment, but Dave was getting worse. The cause of his condition was unknown. We do know that what began as an inflammatory condition in his lung tissue, led quickly to scarring and degraded lung function. At the point that Dave was referred to me it was clearly appropriate that we consider a lung transplant."

Dr. Trulock recalls that Dave scored strongly in the rigorous screening process, including a precise examination of his other vital organs, such as his heart, kidneys and liver. The physician describes the outpatient process that Dave underwent at Barnes as an in-depth on-site battery of test and formal evaluation. All of the results were eventually reviewed by a 50-member panel. At their weekly conference, a subgroup of interdisciplinary specialists including pulmonary physicians, a transplant surgeon, social worker, nurse coordinator, dietitian, pulmonary rehabilitation specialist and psychologist each made a report on the acceptability of the candidate. "The bottom-line questions are pretty straight-forward," Dr. Trulock explains. "Does the patient really need a transplant? Is the patient capable of surviving a transplant? The scarcity of donor organs is a complicating factor that puts a great burden on the decision that the evaluation team makes. We are obliged to select the patients who will benefit most from the procedure, because of our limited resources.

"It's not a socioeconomic decision, but an attempt to be fair and just," adds Dr. Trulock. "For example a street person might really need a lung transplant, but would that person be likely to go back to the stress after a transplant and take the necessary active role in their own care?" At his earliest meetings with Dave and Judy, Dr. Trulock was reassured that the down-to-earth beer hauler and his devoted wife comprised the kind of team that was made-to-order for a successful post-transplant effort. Dave's pulmonary capabilities were progressively degrading, but Dr. Trulock had seen candidates in much worse shape. "He had less than 50 percent lung capacity," the long-time Barnes Hospital physician recalls. "But unlike many patients with severe pulmonary fibrosis who are disabled and often unable to even walk, Dave was ambulatory and not totally incapacitated. He needed some help with bathing and dressing, and he was becoming increasingly oxygen-dependent, but I thought immediately that he would be a good candidate. He seemed to be a very strong-willed man, and I was impressed by the evident bond he had with his wife.

Strong family support is a leading indicator in successful transplant recovery. After the appropriate review by our selection committee, Dave was formally accepted as a candidate for lung transplantation."

Dr. Trulock had no trouble spotting the connection that had strengthened Dave and Judy's lives through separation and tragedy for more than 20 years. But the good news of Dave's acceptance into the Barnes Hospital transplant program was balanced by the growing pressures of Dave's worsening condition. That unchangeable fact and the related deterioration of the Sikes' financial health were beginning to strain at that link in a way that alarmed Dave and Judy.

Judy had tried her best for a year to make her efforts selling insurance and securities pay off for the family as Dave's worsening condition made work impossible for the proud man. Judy actually discovered that she was losing money when she factored in the job requirement to take clients to dinner on a frequent basis. The dynamics of sales simply didn't overlay the modest, by nature reserved, outline of the quiet woman whose shyness, as a youngster, had caused would-be friends to mistakenly characterize her as snobby. "I was worried about our finances, and my concern was constantly communicated to Dave who felt like he was letting us down."

Judy agonized over her decision to give up her insurance brokering business. But growing publicity about Dave's condition — a big article in Millstadt's weekly newspaper detailed Dave's medical and financial dilemma — brought relief and support from unexpected sources, and allowed her to end that unpleasant phase of her work career. Dave's extended leave of absence status with Fritz Distributors left him paying a $500-a-month insurance premium under the COBRA transitional insurance program. The cost of Dave's medications alone, combined with the cost of his high-tech medical care and high-priced physicians threatened the Sikes with a lifetime of debt and worry.

Dave, Judy and the kids had been familiar faces in the Millstadt community for many years. In a small town like Millstadt, faces matter. Smiles and frowns and expressions of worry — subtle signs without the power generally to impact the pace of big city life — have the energy to cause small-town neighbors to stop what they're doing and ask themselves the question, "what's wrong?" Neighbors in Millstadt asked themselves that question about the Sikes'. And when they saw the picture of a troubled Dave and Judy on page 3A of their hometown newspaper as they stopped by Ray's One-Stop to get their morning cup of coffee, they nodded to themselves that it was time to lend a hand. Dave's friends and colleagues in the Millstadt JCs and the VFW organized fund-raisers to defray the Sikes' medical costs. One Saturday afternoon as Judy put together lunch in the kitchen she answered the phone and heard an unfamiliar man's voice on the phone introducing himself as the pastor of Millstadt's only Lutheran church. "Mrs. Sikes our congregation, in some small way, would like to help you and your husband meet the financial challenges that have been placed upon your shoulders by your husband's illness. The vote was unanimous."

"We're not even Lutheran," was Judy's incredulous response. But at this point in Dave's descent into physical helplessness and hacking, ubiquitous discomfort, the Sikes' compounding worries had assumed ecumenical proportions. Still, the fund-raisers were comforting events for the whole community. Friends and neighbors filled up the church basement, and later the VFW's musty beer hall shrine. They shared smiles and hugs and words of encouragement. Dave and Judy fought to overcome their natural reticence to be the center of attention. Dave sat in the middle of the sea of well-wishers, oxygen canister parked on the metal folding chair next to him. He smiled and shook hands with old friends, customers and co-workers, but even that minimum exertion exhausted him. He bowed his head and inhaled mightily to refill his shrinking lungs.

Judy circulated in the room, trying hard to pay attention to the small talk from friends about the weather and the usual gossip about local goings–on, which she calls the "flip side" of small-town togetherness, a sometimes annoying lack of privacy. Out of the corner of her eye she kept tabs on Dave, who seemed to her a small helpless figure in the midst of the churning crowd. As an old girlfriend of Judy's droned on in her ear about the cost of milk at the one major grocery store in town, the devoted wife couldn't stop herself from wondering if Dave would ever again see many of those who had come to pay their respects. The events raised thousands of dollars and temporarily lifted Dave and Judy's spirits, but the unknowable nature of their futures pressed in on them relentlessly.

Despite his confusion about what lay ahead, and the real fear that periodically invaded his thoughts and dreams, Dave's biggest immediate problem was boredom — a sensation unknown to the active man since his days killing time with malaria on a hospital ship in the South China Sea. Now firmly tethered to the oxygen canister that was a more constant companion even than Judy, he struggled to find a sense of purpose. And in that battle for meaning, were sewn the seeds of a physical, emotional and spiritual re-birth.

"You can analyze it with a hundred

psychological terms, but the truth is I just got tired of sitting around," says Dave, in his usual way of explaining profound values with a shrug and simple assertion of fact. "I badly needed a sense of usefulness. I knew I had to move slow, but I figured I had time to do some simple things."

Those basic tasks included housekeeping — washing dishes or dusting — at a pace that would have embarrassed the most feeble, elderly homemaker. He began surprising Judy, as she returned from work stressed and exhausted, with unpretentious meals that he prepared himself. Pizza, steamed vegetables — once, he made a cake for her birthday and joked there was no way he could help her blow out the candles. He attended to his new duties tethered to his oxygen canister, feeling something like one of those old-time deep sea divers he had enjoyed watching in the black and white movies of his childhood. "It's like you're attached to a 50-foot hose — to find Dave you just have to follow the hose," he recalls with a chuckle. By the following summer he had adapted his routine for outside chores by tucking his O2 canister into a backpack. Frustratingly slowly, but inexorably, he would cut the grass, row by meticulous row, with his pack slapping rhythmically against his broad, bare, sweating back.

But that winter, as Dave found new meaning and surprising satisfaction in slowly-executed household activities, he hungered for a more creative outlet to his sense of mission. "In January, we bought a used piano, and I started taking lessons from a lady in town," he says. "Music, playing the piano, had always been something I was interested in, but taking piano lessons as a kid would have probably seemed like a sissy thing to do among the crowd I hung around with. Now, I had the opportunity to do something most people don't have the time to do."

Playing an hour or two a day, Dave took to the keyboard as he had taken to radios, engines and water-softening equipment. He enjoyed the mathematical foundation of musical scales and key changes and appreciated the hand dexterity necessary for success. He exhibited the same good-with-his-hands craftsmanship that had always been his most notable skill. As he performed for Judy, Krista and Randy in the living room of their Millstadt home, swaying gently on the black piano bench to the melody of the theme from Romeo and Juliet, he had evolved into something much more accomplished that a simple craftsman. The music touched his heart at a level of meaning that he had never found with mechanical exercises. No work activity, or even the visceral adrenaline rush of hurling a supercharged motorcycle up a steep hill had ever offered as precious a moment as he felt listening to those rich notes flow from his fingers while his oxygen canister balanced on the bench at his side. A novice pianist, he lacked the experience and polish to play with flawless technique, and an occasional missed note was accented by a sudden twitch of his shoulders, but he played with amazing soul and sensitivity for a beginner. A new, previously hidden face of his personality was revealed to his family as he rose haltingly from his bench, turned slowly and acknowledged their applause with a sheepish smile and a half bow.

Meantime, the monthly trips to St. Louis and Dr. Trulock's office continued. Despite their real dependence on the soft-spoken southerner for any sense of direction about their uncertain future, initially, the Sikes' sense of their standing with Dr. Trulock was that of a strictly professional relationship. "When we first met he seemed cold," says Dave. "Only later, after the transplant did he really warm up."

For his part, the veteran physician explains that a measure of objectivity and impartiality is a critical guideline in an undertaking where an average of 10-12 percent of patients on the lung transplant waiting list die before their opportunity arrives. “I try not to delve into the private lives of patients beyond what they want to volunteer,” he says. “I typically don’t ask questions not relevant to care — and the reality is many patients don’t like to have their privacy invaded.”

Dr. Trulock explains the systematic lung transplant program approach that strives to keep personal preferences out of the process. Candidates on the transplant waiting list receive a sequential number that is based on their acceptance date into the program, not the rate of advancement of their lung disease. In 1994, at the time Dave was receiving treatment as number 81 on the transplant list, he was one of 450 hopeful individuals waiting for a new chance to live. Candidates in the local area are scheduled once a month at Barnes Hospital for follow-up assessment. Out-of-state candidates typically re-locate to the St. Louis area for convenience of care. “Once you’re on the list to receive a donor organ we take on primary care for your disease,” adds Dr. Trulock, referring to his team of inter-disciplinary colleagues who have built the Barnes, Washington University Medical School program into one of the most coveted lung transplant destinations in the world. Despite that impressive assembled expertise, and mortality outcomes that are improving every year, Dr. Trulock concedes that a "lung transplant is treatment, not a cure. It can fail." He cites a study of a statistically significant group of lung transplant recipients from 1990 in which 50 percent of patients lived 5-10 years, with the longest survivor living 14 years.

"For most patients, it's a race against the clock," Dr. Trulock says. "For patients on the list, your life may not be in immediate jeopardy, but the clock is clearly ticking. All of our patients get very tired of waiting. As a patient you have no idea when that donor lung is coming."

Dave , whose musical taste runs toward oldies and the ballads he prefers to play on his living room piano, was nonetheless, in perfect tune with rocker Tom Petty's sentiment that "the waiting is the hardest part."

"We had been on the waiting list for nine months with no calls, but they did decide to give me a pager in June of 1994, which we took as a good sign," Dave says. His sense of boredom had given way to a growing edginess and the skin-prickling realization that time was running out. "We're waiting for the pager to go off, and every false alarm, every time the microwave beeps or the alarm clock goes off, you want to jump out of your skin."

That's saying a lot for a man whose decreasing ability to siphon oxygen from the atmosphere had slowed his reactions, by the summer of 1994, to a stuck-in-quicksand shadow of his former self. The beeper was at once an article of hope and an instrument of incarceration. The Sikes couldn't go more than 25 miles away from their home for fear of traveling out of reach of the call they knew might never come. They were restricted to traveling no further than an hour's drive from Barnes Hospital. The cruelty of their ongoing imprisonment was palpable. They were jailed in their own fear, in their own helplessness, in their own frustration. In Dave's case, he was literally imprisoned in his own respiratory and circulatory systems that were running out of steam. The visible chain that restrained him was the plastic tubing that snaked from his ever-present oxygen canister into his wide nostrils. "People stared at me all the time – even when the tank is hidden in my backpack," he recalls. "I remember a little boy asking his mother, 'why does that man have a string in his nose? In a crowded elevator I'd wonder if people were asking themselves, 'does that man have AIDS?'"

The temptation to be self-absorbed was powerful. The survival instinct prodded Dave toward a self-focus that could have shut him down to his family, his community and everyone he came into contact with. To be selfish at this point in his struggle to live would have been the easiest path, but Dave had never chosen that route before. There were still people depending on him — Judy and Krista, Mom, and another group of people he had just met.

The members of the Lung Transplant Support Group were mostly folks in the same tough situation as Dave. Once a week, Dave and Judy made the drive to St. Louis and Barnes Hospital for a meeting. Usually, Judy was at the wheel, because even the relatively passive task of driving had become a tiring chore for Dave. The meetings consisted mostly of newly accepted members to the lung transplant recipient list introducing themselves and describing their very personal struggles. Sometimes a hesitant, most-often middle-aged man or woman would stand up and describe how they had made the trip down from Nebraska, or up from Arkansas. "We're staying at the Barnes Lodge (the 20-room facility operated on the medical center campus by Barnes

Hospital for patients and families outside a 50-mile radius)," they'd say, or maybe, "We rented a room down in the Central West End — awful hot here, but the doctors and nurses have been real nice."

When Dave introduced himself he remained seated and slowly began sharing his story from the point when he first doubled over on the racquetball court and grabbed his heaving chest. At one point after he introduced Judy and referenced daughter Krista, he veered onto a path that surprised Judy and brought a tear to her eye. "Our oldest daughter Kerri was killed in car accident three years ago," he said in the steady monotone he maintained when forced to speak in a public setting. "She was a beautiful girl, and she made everybody smile who ever met her," he added, looking down at the conference table in front of him. A lone tear dropped to the polished surface. "Even when she died she was giving to others, because she signed her driver's license and became an organ donor. I never thought I'd be here talking to a group of people like me who are depending on a stranger to give that same gift to one of us." When Judy looked around the table, tears were flowing all around.

Dave and Judy took great comfort from the stories of others. They were equally moving. But it was concrete medical information they hungered for most. Sometimes that came from a medical professional serving as a guest speaker, a pulmonologist, a social worker, best of all a transplant surgeon. Often the source was another patient in the program who had taken the initiative to do the research.

While they valued the information tremendously, the knowledge was sometimes unsettling. The prospect of a lifetime battle against Dave's own immune system in response to an invading foreign object — a new lung or lungs — was daunting. "We asked ourselves are we trading one disease for another — knowing that my immune system would be devastated by the anti rejections drugs," Dave explains. "A lot of people, facing this future, would probably look at the process and decide they'd rather wait to die." But the interaction within the support group, despite the nearly overwhelming time and health pressures facing each group member, wasn't all doom and gloom by any means. "I met people in the program who were really fun," he says. "There was a guy from Florida, who was here for a year, staying in a town house over on Lindel. "We got to know one another at the support group meeting, but we began to visit each other's homes."

Neil Kauten was a salesman and the kind of outgoing character who impressed Dave , mild-mannered former Marine, by having the brass to loudly insist the bartender change channels on the TV in a crowded St. Louis restaurant while they waited for lunch to arrive. The mismatched friends even played a couple of rounds of slow-motion golf that summer, while they waited for the reprieve that might never come. On the last day of June in 1994, Dave's new buddy got his lung transplant, and Dave felt the same bittersweet emotion he had know in Vietnam when a squadmate got the word he was shipping out. "I was happy for him, but it made me a little anxious about my own number coming up."

For Judy, the battle to stay focused on Dave's illness and remain positive about the future had an unforeseen benefit. "It forced me to focus on him and get beyond some of the grief I was carrying around for Kerri," she says. There were times when this preoccupation with her husband wasn't a sturdy enough shield against the cutting hurt. Mother's Day and Kerri's birthday were the worst days of the year for Judy, who began a new job in March working for the Illinois-American Water Company. On these occasions special memories would force themselves in. Memories like the time, on Judy's 40th birthday, when Kerri taped a "Happy Birthday Mom" sign to the back of the family van. Judy couldn't figure out why other drivers were honking and waving at her until one driver hollered "happy birthday". When she got out of the van, she saw the sign and knew instantly who had taped it there.

But it was a noticeable change in Dave's attitude that most captured Judy's attention and jolted her out of her reveries. Dave had decided to fight back against his illness. "It was encouraging — kind of inspiring — to see him doing things again that made him happy and feeling useful," she says.

Whether it was conducting a living room concert for Judy and Krista on the piano, baking a caramel-frosted cake or sending away for Spanish tapes to learn the language he had butchered in high school, Dave returned to a simple guiding principle. It was one that had always directed him, but which he had temporarily lost in the confusion, fear and exhaustion surrounding his progressing disease. He set goals. A goal for each day, each week, each month. Some of those milestones involved a simple tangible achievement like getting the grass cut over a three-day period. But others dealt with a side of his deepest self that

Dave had rarely revealed even to Judy and his daughters.

Until Kerri's death, Dave had taken it for granted that God was on his side. That event, didn't shake his essential belief in the man upstairs, but persuaded Dave that just maybe God didn't always pay attention. Maybe the Lord had been dealing with some other vital crisis on that terrible night, some decision or request that could change the world for countless millions. He couldn't have meant for beautiful Kerri to die that way, had to be something that slipped through.

For a while, Dave had withdrawn from God as he had withdrawn from the rest of the world. But after dealing with the initial shock of his own illness and the very real possibility that he, too, was going to die, Dave became gradually convinced that a divine hand that was conducting events toward a meaningful conclusion. And that Kerri's death was somehow connected to his own personal journey and search for understanding. There was some reason for her death and his sickness. He needed to find it.

He began to pray again — daily, at greater length and more fiercely than he had ever prayed before. Dave wasn't satisfied this time to let God off the hook. He didn't want to continue down this short path to his own destruction without understanding why he was going there. Each day he asked God that question. Why? And while no clear response came like a thunderbolt from heaven, the faithful son, husband, Marine and father thought he got a partial answer one day in his partner's eyes. They were red and puffy from crying — maybe about him, maybe about Kerri. It didn't matter. He had always found the truth in those eyes, and now they — God — revealed Dave's mandate with profound clarity. The simple condition for sharing in the Lord's plan for him was to do his part. To never give up. To carry out his responsibilities to help the people who were suffering with him. To be as alive as he possibly could within the breaking-down body that confined his blooming spirit. Part of that meant going to his transplant support group sessions and comforting others. It also required him to remain hopeful that his transplant number would eventually be called.

Judy didn't know where the changes came from, she just thanked God for bringing back the man she had loved for more than 30 years, and helping him to grow. "Suddenly he was more giving than he had ever been in our marriage," she recalls, touching her husband's hand as she describes those challenging days. "He had an appreciation for the beauty in nature and day-to-day life that I had never seen before. I felt as though God had given me the husband every woman dreams of. Dave was learning a little Spanish from his self-help tapes, and we talked about the exotic places we'd visit after Dave got his transplant."

There was no way of knowing when the call would come that could make those dreams possible. A support group friend from Granite City, Illinois, did get the call and his transplant went well. "The waiting was horrible, and it was worse because I really began to feel good about my chances for success with the transplant," explains Dave. "I thought to myself, 'maybe it does work.' Still, you keep on waiting, hoping the call will come before it's too late. Every morning when I woke up I began asking God, 'will it be my turn today?'"

Christmas 1994 was a low point for the Sikes family. Dave's overall energy level was sinking fast. His portable oxygen supply failed to compensate for his diminished lung capacity. Dave describes the excruciating sensation of suffocating with every labored breath. "I felt like I was walking on thin ice waiting to fall into the pond and dip below the ice waters where I wouldn't be able to breathe." Frequently, Dave's violent coughing fits overwhelmed Andy Williams' or Nat King Cole's smooth melodies on the CD player.

The fresh scent of the recently cut Christmas tree mixed with sugar cookies baking in the oven, but Dave, transparent plastic tubing disappearing into his nose like dual trains into a dark tunnel, could smell none of it. After a particularly rough coughing spasm, Judy would beat on his back to dislodge the flem from his lungs.

In the deep winter of 1994 and 1995, Dave' existence had evolved into a shadow life where all motion, and finally, even coherent thinking, slowed to an almost imperceptible rate. The spiritual revival that had begun in the summer was all but overcome by the physical decline that sprang from Dave's basic inability to take in life-affirming air. The energy even to pray was slowly deserting him. There was simply no fuel to generate the power to propel his legs, or increasingly his thoughts. "I would walk 30 feet from my chair to my bedroom and cough violently for a half an hour," Dave recalls. "It was like being in Vietnam again, waiting to die, and wondering if your next day on earth might be your last." As in Vietnam, an occasional joke and a smile from Dave would penetrate the thick tension.

Once, as he leaned back in his chair, absently watching a football game on the television, he jokingly remarked to Krista's boyfriend Randy that the youngster might inherit Dave's favorite recliner if he hung around. No one except Dave smiled at the black quip, but Dave had always met fear with humor. He didn't want his family to waste their holidays worrying about him. Dave got a call from Father Neff, the priest and longtime family friend. Father Neff encouraged Dave not to lose hope and to hold on to the strength that had always stood as a strong foundation for his family.

The Sikes' vigil waiting for new lungs was approaching two years — by lung transplant standards, a very long time. Dave could hardly walk. He wasn't afraid to die, but frustrated that he might not get the chance to put his new interests and new outlook to work creating a better life for Judy and Krista. Krista and Randy had become engaged that Christmas. Randy would do fine making sure that pretty Krista was safe and happy but Dave was afraid he would never be able to walk her down the aisle.

What about Judy? She was still young, still beautiful. He hated to think, even for a fleeting instant, of her with another man, but maybe that would be for the best. He wanted her to be happy and her life had always been full of love. "God, look after her," he prayed, one night in his bed struggling to sleep and escape the drowning sensation that gripped his chest and moved down into his legs. He wasn't sure if he had said the words out loud.

That short prayer was about all he could manage. He seemed to remember a mission he had undertaken to get close enough to God to understand why all this was happening, and to know for sure that he would see Kerri when he got to where he was going. But he was too tired to think about that now. Judy was talking to him about going back to church. They hadn't been good about going to church since Kerri died. The surroundings reminded them so acutely of their daughter, first communion, that terrible cold day when they buried her. It wasn't church exactly she was talking about. Something like, "we need as much help as we can get."

As she watched her husband disappearing before her eyes, with no sign of relief from the medical experts in whose care and hopeful projections they had put so much faith, Judy frantically grasped for another option. In early January 1995, a friend named Chuck Renner, whom Judy had met while selling insurance, shared with her a prayer to St. Anthony, known even to Catholic convert Judy as the patron saint of the sick. Chuck explained that some devout Catholics professed faith in a healing prayer formula that required the petitioner to place nine copies of the prayer at a special holy place nine weeks in a row.

"Sorry honey, I don't think I've got nine weeks," Dave slowly responded as he struggled to comprehend Judy's plan. Still he was too tired and increasingly light headed from the lack of oxygen to argue the point. She was looking for a holy place. Dave remembered a place that Clara had brought him to as a child. She had knelt outside and said her rosary. It was the place where the Holy Mother had appeared.

The next thing he knew, Dave found himself in the passenger seat next to Judy as she drove down Highway 15 on the evening of Jan. 5 toward the shrine of Our Lady of the Snows in south Belleville, Illinois. Famous for its Christmas season light and nativity presentations, the shrine attracted pilgrims in search of a more spiritual experience year-round.

Dave and Judy were among that company of the faithful looking for nothing less than a miracle. Judy parked the Ford Probe at the designated lot — a good walk away from the shrine where the Blessed Virgin is said to have appeared to some local believers at the turn of the century. Judy worried about Dave's ability to make the walk. It was late afternoon and the first shadows of darkness were deepening on the horizon. She helped him out of the car and allowed him to use her shoulder as a crutch as they moved haltingly across the parking lot and onto the brown grass path that led to the shrine. Sparse patches of icy snow dotted the ground, and Judy led them carefully forward, asking Dave at what seemed like every fifth step how he was feeling. "Fine," Dave said, and although his breathing was labored and his pace slow, there was something about the urgency with which he gripped her arm that led Judy to believe he was alert and excited about reaching their destination.

They found the shrine in the middle of a grotto, surrounded by tall Oaks and Birches that constituted a silent congregation around the shrine. Silent except for the faint whispers of a light wind that jostled the bare branches above their heads where they knelt. A few other human visitors stood around the shrine, but they must have completed their devotions, or else they noticed the urgency as

Dave and Judy approached the marble alter cut into the rock where the Mother of God had revealed herself. Those gathered around the shrine noticed, in the slightly bowed man with the backpack and the tubes leading into his nose, a sudden lightening of his unseen load as he moved quickly to the alter. With more agility than they expected, he dropped his partner's arm and fell on his own to his knees. He bowed his head and began to pray earnestly.

The blonde woman with him rose and took a match from her purse. She lit both altar candles and gently nestled some pieces of paper under one of the heavy brass candlestands. She fell back to her knees beside the man who had accompanied her and grasped his hand tightly. And now it seemed to some who had witnessed the whole scene unfold as if it were the woman who was gaining strength from the touch of her partner. Darkness descended around the couple.

"I felt very peaceful there," recalls Judy with a smile that reflects the insignificance of verbal description in the face of the sacred. "At that time Dave moved very slowly, but it felt as though the whole world was revolving in slow motion. All of my senses were heightened."

Dave adds simply, "I knew it was up to

him. I needed help that no doctor could give me." Like Judy, a literal description of the events on that later January afternoon escapes him. But today, more than 8 years after he knelt, near death, in that grotto and bowed his head, Dave believes that it was in that blessed place that God gave him the answer he had been looking for.

The Sikes made five more trips to Our Lady of the Snows Shrine, each time leaving their copies of the prayer to St. Anthony. Finally, Dave was unable to walk on his own at all. February 1995 began and the end, for Dave, seemed near. Fortunately, miracles, as the Sikes will tell you first-hand, are sometimes just a phone call away.

A Breath of Fresh Air

When the pager went off at 6 a.m. on Feb. 8, 1995, the Sikes' first reaction — after shaking off the cobwebs of a restless sleep — was fear. Could this be just another false alarm? There had been the Christmas Eve wrong number — scornful in its broken promise of hope, its sharp reminder that this might be Dave's last Christmas. Dave was slowly dying of a disease that was eating away his lungs. He had a rare form of chronic lung disease called idiopathic fibrosis, and nobody knew how he got it. Like the night the call came in about Kerri, the Sikes were in bed. Returning Barnes Hospital's page, Judy dialed the phone. The woman on the other end asked for Dave. "Mr. Sikes, we may have a lung donor for you. Can you come in immediately?"

"Okay, okay, sure," Dave responded with the same indifferent tone he would have affected to answer a telemarketer's query about his choice in soaps. Except Dave's right hand shook slightly as he held the phone and his heart skipped a beat. The former Marine, who had looked death in the eye before, sensed this was going to be his last best chance to live.

Dave took a quick shower and pulled on a loose-fitting sweat suit. After more than a year of battling his energy-draining disease, comfort was a dim memory. Even then, anticipating the prospect of finally receiving the lung transplant that was his only hope, with all the excitement and fear that was driving his racing heart, Dave was prepared to wait. Waiting had become a way of life.

But at that moment, the Sikes were moving faster than they had moved in some time. They were out the door by 6:30 a.m. It was a cold, clear day.

Judy got behind the wheel of their Ford Probe. She shifted the seat up close to the dashboard and jabbed the stick into reverse. In her nervousness, she ground the gears backing out of the driveway. "Would you like me to drive?" Dave asked with a smile that broke the tension a little.

Finally, they were on the road — rural highways winding through familiar farmland, past coalmines and the small Illinois towns of Cahokia and Sauget. Hungry for divine intervention, they were nevertheless oblivious to a favorite spiritual landmark as they drove by lost in their thoughts — the white steeple of the 100-year-old Concordia Church pointed heavenward off Route 163. From 163, they took 157, north on Route 3, to the

Interstate 40 on-ramp, over the Mississippi River on the Poplar Street Bridge heading west.

Judy drove carefully, occasionally grasping Dave's hand and smiling. "We both knew this could be our last drive together," she recalls. Dave, ever-present oxygen cylinder at his side, weakly pulled precious air, which his failing lungs would no longer produce, through the cannula plugged into his nose. Plastic tubing snaked from the six-liter oxygen tank, wrapped around his ears, and anchored at the base of his nostrils in a circuitous trail that routinely drew amazed stares from children and some adults.

Now in the car, moving toward an uncertain future, Dave wasn't thinking about the possibility of his own death. He was pondering, for the first time, the fact that someone else had died suddenly to launch his race to the hospital. "It was in the back of my mind that someone I didn't know was my only chance to live," he says. "And I would never know that person, because he or she was dead."

The real possibility that this opportunity might still turn out to be a dud was more frightening to Dave than the thought that he might not survive the transplant. "I had waited so long for this day to happen — a year-and-a-half, dying a little at a time," he says. "Judy and I knew that we could get all the way to the hospital, get ready for the operation, and something might go wrong. They could send us home without the transplant." The fortunate orphan, who found deliverance in the arms of his adoptive parents and cheated death in the jungles of Vietnam, says simply of that possibility, "I don't know if I could have gone on."

Dave was no doctor, but his intense experience in the Barnes Hospital Lung Transplant Program had transformed the onetime indifferent student into a lay expert on lung disease. He understood implicitly the diverse factors that make lung transplants relatively rare. Less than half the number of lung transplants are performed compared with heart, kidney and liver procedures.

Challenges such as matching lung sizes and harvesting the organs quickly to overcome rapid tissue deterioration after death mean that transplant teams are only able to harvest one set of lungs from every 10 donors. That's why Dave had been tied for more than three months to a pager that limited his travel to within 30 minutes driving time of Barnes Hospital. These issues, combined with another complicating factor — the low availability of rare AB-negative blood that Dave would need for his radical surgery — reminded him that his odds for success were still a bad bet.

But as the mile markers blurred by, and he struggled to inhale enough oxygen to keep him alive for another minute, another hour, another day, Dave glanced at Judy behind the wheel, fighting hard through the fear to keep things together. Even now, in the make-do blouse and pants she had thrown on, with her blonde hair mussed a little, the soft morning sunshine lit her face in a way he had seen before and always loved. Yes, this transplant was worth the risk. He thought about his only surviving daughter, Krista, back at work in Illinois, searching for her own identity in the world after losing the big sister she had idolized and emulated. Their perseverance provided the example. This chance for life meant everything to Dave . It was the only one he had.

They took the exit at Kingshighway Boulevard, where Barnes Hospital rose from St. Louis' Central West End, 17 stories into the early morning haze. Among the many fortunate circumstances of the Sikes' lives together was their proximity to one of the nation's great hospitals. Millstadt, Ill., may be a small farming town in

America's heartland with modest resources and unassuming neighbors, but Dave 's home lay in the shadow of a special place where healers used technology and skill to accomplish miracles.

Barnes, today Barnes-Jewish Hospital, after a 1996 merger, is the teaching hospital for Washington University's School of Medicine. It's also a major transplant center for heart, kidneys and livers, but its prominence as a world leader in lung transplants gave Dave and Judy hope for life after Dave's lung disease brought their existence to a cruel standstill.

As Dave ' family prospered in rural Illinois in the 1980s, without any thought of the hardships ahead, Barnes' lung transplant program evolved into one of the best of its kind in the world. The capability to replace failing, diseased lungs with healthy harvested donor organs was pioneered in Toronto, Canada, by a team of surgeons, including Dr. Joel Cooper. Cooper performed the first successful human lung transplant in 1983 at the University of Toronto, before bringing his expertise to St. Louis in 1988. In 1989, Cooper and his Barnes Hospital, Washington University colleagues advanced the state of lung transplant art another notch. They perfected a technique, called sequential bilateral transplant, in which a patient 's diseased lungs are replaced — one at a time — by healthy donor lungs. Previously, a double lung transplant involved the simultaneous replacement of both diseased lungs with donor lungs — a trickier challenge, inviting complications.

With the arrival at Barnes of Cooper's surgical colleague and fellow Canadian Dr. Alec Patterson, in 1991, the momentum of lung transplantation in St. Louis picked up steam. Since those heady days of the late 1980s and early 1990s, nearly 700 adult patients have received lung transplants at Barnes-Jewish Hospital. Just a block away from Barnes-Jewish, on the Washington University Medical Center campus, St. Louis Children's Hospital has become a world leader in lung transplants for kids.

As she turned right off of Kingshighway Boulevard squinting in the early morning glare, Judy was less focused on Barnes' worldwide reputation as a lung transplant center than on its traffic-congested campus and limited parking. She dropped Dave off at the hospital's front entrance and parked the Probe in an underground lot. After taking the elevator to the sixth floor, where transplant patients are prepped for the grueling ordeal ahead, Dave was met by specially trained nurses who constitute part of the multidisciplinary transplant team. Dave was in his hospital gown by the time Judy returned from admissions. He was in a preparation area that felt more like a meat locker to him than a hospital room. The temperature seemed unusually cold to the excited patient whose broad backside was only thinly insulated by his drab green hospital garment. He joked with the pretty nurse inserting an intravenous line into his arm that he could see her breath.

During their long stay in the holding room, the Sikes were alert to the dreaded possibility that they might be involved in a dry run. They had been told the potential donor was someone who had been killed in a car crash in Georgia. "We knew the whole thing could be shot down with one word," says Judy. The lungs might not be a match, they might not be the right size. Would the family give their permission, as the Sikes had done four years earlier?

Judy called Krista about 9:30 a.m. She could tell from her daughter's voice that the 21-year-old was having a brutal day at her new job at American Water Works in Belleville. Judy asked Krista to explain the situation to her boss and come to the hospital. Judy sensed — despite the real potential that any number of factors could derail the operation — that the moment of no-return was at hand. It would take time for Krista to get to Barnes. She must have the chance to see her Dad before he goes under, Judy thought. Her mind flashed instantly to Kerri's smile the last time she saw her daughter alive. Judy called Dave's sister Jean Marie in Belleville and told her to join them.

Soon after that call, a smiling nurse sprang into the room and proclaimed excitedly, "The lungs are on their way from Atlanta."

Attendants transported the sedated patient on a cart to the second-floor surgical unit where transplants are conducted. Judy and the newly arrived Krista waited behind, eyes brimming with tears, feeling utterly helpless. Krista had gotten lost on her way to the hospital, but she had arrived in time to hold her Dad's hand and tell him she loved him.

An anesthesiologist prepared to insert an epidural into Dave's spine. Judy and Krista had rejoined Dave in a small prep room adjacent to the OR. This transplant is really going to happen, the Sikes family dared to believe. The physician carefully examined the taut skin between Dave's spinal vertebrae into which he would jab the hollow needle dripping with fluid to desensitize most of Dave's upper torso. A nurse joked that it was time for Dave to "get his margarita now." When Dave said he was ready for them to put the needle in his back, another nurse responded, "it's already in." A phone rang faintly somewhere in another room. Softly, without a trace of sarcasm, Dave said, "I'll get it."

Before Dave fully lost consciousness, Dr. Patterson walked in. Alec Patterson M.D., professor of surgery and cardiothoracic surgery at Washington University School of Medicine, is the world-renowned lung transplant surgeon who would operate on Dave. He moved his practice to St. Louis in the early 1990s after helping to pioneer the procedure in his hometown of Toronto. He is well over six-foot tall, almost imposing for a doctor, with light brown, longish hair and a slight Canadian inflection to his measured speech. "You're getting a bonus," he told Dave, who was half-listening. "We're going to give you two healthy lungs from a 15-year-old girl. They're a little bit smaller than yours."

The prospect of one of the girl's smallish lungs powering his broad-shouldered patient had struck the experienced transplant surgeon as problematic. He had quickly changed plans from a single lung transplant to the double lung option. Flexibility and a calm comfort level with unpredictable events were routine elements of Dr. Patterson's highly irregular world. The soft-spoken Canadian appreciated the irony of his occupation. A lung transplant was a precise, exacting exercise totally dependent on the whims of fate. The same whims of fate — in Dave's mind, the will of God — had brought the 45-year-old patient to this precarious moment in time.

Despite his diminished capacities, a memory echoed in Dave's mind at the mention of his donor's age. A young girl killed in a car accident. He was getting a bonus, he thought the doctor had said. Two for the price of one, but what a price! Another young life lost, another father 's daughter. Dr. Patterson asked if they had any questions, and Dave and Judy could summon none. The time for questions was over. It was time, finally, to act.

They were ready to take Dave into the operating room. Despite his sedation, Judy remembers her husband's eyes getting big. She thought he was scared. Strangely, Judy felt a sense of peace at the moment when she could no longer do anything to help. She had been there for him at every moment of his illness, literally a fortified shoulder for him to lean on as his own strength had waned and ultimately disappeared. Now, she watched the transplant team take Dave away, and she could do nothing but pray. She remembered the candles they had lit together at Our Lady of the Snows shrine in Belleville only weeks before. "I don't know why, but I had a feeling God was going with him into that room. I felt only positive feelings. I had confidence in our faith, in Dr. Patterson, and I knew somehow I would be taking Dave home." Dave entered the operating room about 12:30 p.m.

At 12:45, Dave was lying on the operating table while a scrub nurse assembled instruments on a smaller table at the foot of his operating station. He was unconscious, a passive bystander in the surgical ballet that was about to unfold. The temperature in the OR was 66 degrees. On top of the sterile blue cloth that covered the instrument table, the nurse carefully arranged an intricate selection of surgical tools. These included retractors and forceps of various sizes, clamps, suction devices and small suturing tools to manipulate and place thin surgical thread that would be used to sew up Dave's incisions.

Another nurse intubated Dave, that is, she guided a long tube through his mouth into his trachea to open an airway for the seven hours that Dave would be under anesthesia. The same tube also provided internal access to sensors — a transesophageal echocardiogram — that offered accurate, redundant recordings of Dave's heart function to the anesthesiologists who gathered near a bank of monitors at the head of the operating table.

The circulation nurse shaved his pubic area, handling the razor quickly and confidently as if she were shaving her own legs. She inserted a catheter into his penis. The proud, modest man would have cringed with embarrassment if he had possessed the power to rise above the operating table and look down upon the scene. But he was aware of nothing, silent to the world except for faint beeping of the monitors that registered his heartbeat and blood pressure.

At 1:15, Dr. Patterson and an assisting surgeon entered the OR after scrubbing up. A nurse helped them squeeze their still-moist hands into latex gloves. Along with the cloth surgical masks that obscured their faces below their eyes, the surgeons sported miniature flashlights fixed at the center of their foreheads by a headband that circled and crisscrossed their blue hairnets. A white tube ran up their necks and over their heads. Dave's chest had been swabbed down with an iodine mixture that left his skin an unnatural hue of pale yellow.

The surgical field, Dave's chest, had been isolated as a yellow square amid the blue surgical cloth that covered the rest of his body from the waist down. After drawing the pattern with a marker, they began to cut into Dave's chest with small high-tech scalpels, called cutting and coagulating devices. Like tiny, extremely precise soldering guns, the instruments opened up tissue while cauterizing the flesh at the same time. There was little blood as the surgeons traced their pattern carefully, but steadily. The acrid odor of burnt meat wafted up from the incisions. The cutting tools released a bit of smoke as they burned through flesh.

Soft jazz music piped into the cold room, offering a musical melody to the sporadic bursts of conversation among the surgical team. "What's his BP?" Patterson asked the anesthesiologist. "Give me an O silk stitch," he softly commanded the scrub nurse. Soft light streaming from a powerful bank of overhead lamps formed a halo around the surgeons' heads. The entire operating table was bathed in a diffused glow.

With the double lung procedure — instead of making his incision through the back as with a single-lung transplant — Patterson exposed Dave's lungs through two incisions: an 18-inch cut across his breastplate and another smaller incision across his sternum. The ex-Marine's arms were tied up behind his back, prisoner-of-war-style, to prevent any involuntary interference with the procedure. Patterson's assistant used a small handsaw to hack through Dave's ribs. The dreadful sound of a serrated blade ripping through human bone wasn't something anyone in the OR noticed two stainless steel clamps held the flaps of Dave's dissected chest open and accessible to the surgeons. They plunged into the gaping cavity up to their elbows with flashing instruments and blood absorbing gauze.

Dr. Patterson was comfortable with the double-lung option for Dave because of his own experience with the procedure and because he knew the clock was running out on his patient.

"We transplant patients who are likely to die within the next year to 18 months," Dr. Patterson explains. "In this case, we didn't have that kind of time."

At 2:30 in the afternoon, as Dave lay profoundly unaware on his back with his chest opened up like a car hood and his pulmonary artery clamped to stop the blood flow and clear the way for the removal of his blackened, shriveled lungs, time seemed to stop.

A beaming operating room technician enters the OR with an ordinary cooler that you might buy at any hardware store or Wal-Mart's. On a hot summer afternoon at the church picnic back in Millstadt, it would have kept Dave's Miller High Life's icy cold. The circulating nurse takes the cooler and opens it up. Before she can release the healthy, gelatinous organs from their two ice-packed plastic bag containers, Patterson shouts,

"How they look?"

"Great," the nurse responds. Nice and pink."

Nodding his head, Patterson reaches into Dave's chest and pulls out one of his atrophied lungs. He has already severed the three main connecting vessels – the airway, the pulmonary artery and the pulmonary vein. Dave's damaged lung has the color and consistency of charcoal after it gets wet and loses its shape. Dark and fibrous, Patterson hands the shrunken organ over to the scrub nurse. "The airway is hard to the touch," he lectures the surgical team, who have heard this analysis before. "Check out the damage – nearly total loss of function." The nurse snips tissue samples from the old lung – including the lymph nodes – for pathology tests in the lab. A small, blood-spotted section of one of Dave's ribs lies discarded on a table next to the other refuse of this assault on his body.

Patterson grabs a handful of ice from a nearby machine that churns ice continually, maintaining the half-frozen H2O at a moderated temperature that won't freeze the donor lungs when they're inserted into Dave's body. Patterson packs Dave's chest cavity with the right amount of slush. Slush machine is even what the transplant team calls the contraption. By now, after many transplants, Patterson can do it by feel.

The nurse hands one of the new lungs to Patterson. He handles it almost casually, with deft confidence, despite the ice and the amorphous nature of the organ. "These will do quite nicely," he says.

He elevates the lung as a priest would elevate the host at the time of consecration, revealing it to the rest of the transplant team in the room. "This is a good specimen -- the team in Atlanta did a good job," he says. "Little or no deterioration."

Gently now, even reverently, Dr. Patterson places the new lungs, one by one, where Dave's old lungs had struggled to supply his body with air. Patterson spreads the slush evenly around the new lungs, occasionally dipping an oversized syringe into the snow-cone-like mixture and basting the lungs with cool liquid. He is ready to begin the intricate process of re-attaching the vessels and arteries that connect Dave's lungs to the rest of his respiratory system.

At 5 in the afternoon, after a great deal of painstaking, delicate work in which the surgical tools pass quickly, sometimes wordlessly, between the surgeons and the scrub nurse, Patterson is ready to perfuse the lung. He snaps up a retractor backhanded. He reopens the pulmonary artery blood spigot and gives Dave's new lungs their first critical test. "How are the vitals?" Patterson asks the anesthesiologist to confirm the conclusion that his own instincts are on target.

"Holding steady. BP's shallowing out a little, but nothing to worry about," the anesthesiologist fires back.

Patterson knows there will be plenty to worry about in the next few days and for many months to come while his patient's body strives to attack the invader tissue in its midst.

It's 5:45, and one critical step remains in the surgical checklist that will send Dave back to the recovery room with the capability of taking a full breath of air for the first time in two years. Patterson carefully re-connects the airway of Dave's new lungs to his larger respiratory system. The ventilator is now pumping oxygen directly into the donor lungs – lungs that less than 24 hours previously gave breath to the energetic strivings of a young Georgia girl. The lungs inflate perfectly. Patterson and his assistant shake latex-gloved hands.

Patterson's assistant closed Dave up -- reversing the previous process with hundreds of sutures that would leave two lasting, tangible symbol of the life-saving experience that Dave would never be able to describe — a couple of gruesome scars.

Dr. Patterson grabbed a shower and a cup of coffee. He prepared his thoughts to complete the day's activities with another challenging task. He would talk to the patient's wife, which was a part of the job he enjoyed a little less than the technical intricacies of lung transplantation.

The Gift

Judy passed agonizing hours in the surgery waiting room. She alternatively sat, paced, watched TV and chatted aimlessly with Krista and Dave's sister Jean. At 2:30 p.m., a nurse announced that one lung was out and a donor lung was going in. Hours crept along with no new news. About 7:30 p.m., Dr. Patterson entered the room. He was no longer in scrubs, but wearing his white lab coat. He looked fresh, rejuvenated. The surgeon greeted Judy with a reassuring smile "Dave's doing fine," Dr. Patterson says in a calm tone, as if performing a double lung transplant was equivalent to applying a few stitches to a cut. "He has two very healthy new lungs," Dr. Patterson adds. Judy hugged the reserved surgeon, who bent his six-foot-plus frame awkwardly to Judy's embrace. The Canadian was uncomfortable, but not surprised by the injection of raw emotion into his orderly environment. "He has been taken to the ICU, and you can see him in about an hour," he says.

When Judy saw Dave in the Intensive Care Unit, she was taken aback by Dr. Patterson's description of "fine." Dave had been fitted with a special pair of sunglasses to protect his eyes. After more than 12 hours under sedation, bright lights might have damaged his eyes when he woke up because of an inability to blink. Ventilation tubes protruded from his mouth and nose, and drainage tubes exited both sides. "With those goggles and all those tubes, he was quite a sight," recalls Judy. Quickly, her original shock was replaced by a profound sense of relief. Judy was accompanied by Krista — both were decked in gowns, hairnets, masks and booties. They carefully approached Dave's bed. Suddenly, they realized that the husband and father they loved had already undergone an amazing transformation. His color had changed markedly. "Before his surgery he had been gray," says Judy. "Now his skin was looking healthy and pink. Just that improvement made me gasp and cry."

Dave slowly stirred. He made a few untranslatable noises, and Judy kissed him on the cheek with the same gentle touch she had bestowed only four years earlier on her dead daughter. The parallels were unavoidable even at this moment of joy and relief for Judy and Krista, but the tears that burned their eyes were tears of joy this time.

The next day, as Dave gradually emerged from the anesthesia-induced blackness, he became aware of ICU staff leaning hard on his chest, attempting to yank the ventilator out of his mouth. Images of Judy and Krista, and even Kerri, flickered on the fringes of his morphine-clouded consciousness.

When he finally looked up into Judy's face, able to see his partner's blue eyes clearly for the first time after the many hours of surgery and halting re-emergence into awareness, Dave believed that he had been reborn into a beautiful new world. It was as if he was seeing Judy again for the first time, like she appeared to him as a schoolgirl in 1967. Yes, he could really breathe, for the first time in more than two years. But in addition to the wonderful sensation of taking a deep breath, the fresh air filling Dave's new lungs oxygenated the blood flowing in his veins. The energy transformed more than the color in his cheeks. The whole world seemed brighter, more vivid, imbued with vibrant colors for a man who 24 hours earlier had looked into the black face of death.

Twenty-four hours after his double lung transplant Dave took his first tentative steps in the direction of his new life. "At first, it was true baby steps — barely moving while I dragged bottles and tubes," Dave recalls. "All the time, I was thinking I'd rather lay down. Man, I just got cut." Instead, Dave listened to his physicians and recovery team, just as he had done as a good Marine. Initially, those orders entailed quick trips around the ICU area. After 10-15 minutes of slow walking, Dave was exhausted.

Dave pondered his lucky number as the 254th lung transplant patient at Barnes Hospital often as he lay in bed in the ICU unit listening to the steady beep of the heart monitor that regularly testified to his new life. "When you think about all the factors falling in line from the first event to the last — someone had to die, her lungs had to be the right size, she had to be close enough that her lungs could be harvested in time and transported in a few hours," he says. "Finally her blood type had to match my AB-negative blood type and her family had to agree to donate her lungs. When you think about all those coincidences, you understand why I know it was more than Dr. Patterson's great skill and my own good fortune that saved my life. Just like back in Vietnam, the man upstairs was looking over my shoulder. There had to be more for me to accomplish. And my transplant number

– number 254 – Kerri had been born on September 11th, the 254th day of the year."

Five days after his transplant Dave was taken back to the sixth floor to continue his recovery, only to suffer a temporary setback. In a reaction that's not uncommon to patients with new donor organs, Dave's heart rate and pulse accelerated dangerously while he was walking – reaching a rate of 172 beats per minute. He was sent to the critical care unit, a level between intensive care and the surgical recovery floor. Judy, who spent all of her available time at the hospital with Dave, witnessed the frightening incident. "The scariest thing about it was I thought he was having a heart attack," she recalls. "I could literally feel his heart jumping out of his chest. We couldn't believe that after all the obstacles Dave overcame to get his new lungs that a simple heart attack would kill him."

During his stay in critical care, while his heart rate was stabilized by medication, Dave's perspective began to turn noticeably inward. "I don't want people standing around watching me have a heart attack," Dave tells Judy. His wife, daughter and sister are Dave's only regular visitors and they all noticed his demeanor change. Although Judy was concerned by his changing moods, she understood the frustration that was gripping both she and her husband by the heart. They were impatient for Dave to recover. After the miracle of his successful lung transplant, small setbacks carried added weight.

But there was something else weighing on Dave's recovery and peace of mind. Something that had been seeping into his consciousness since the call came through that a possible donor had been found. Judy was in a chair at Dave's side in her usual place when she looked up from a magazine to see an unexpected sight. The man she had known intimately for nearly 30 years, and whom she had rarely ever seen cry, was sobbing and wiping away tears that wouldn't stop. Judy sprang to her husband's side and attempted to comfort him, but the source of those tears couldn't be dammed by a mere hug. They were tears of understanding, tears of knowledge. They were the tears of a father whose beloved daughter willingly gave part of herself in death to heal the life of another she would never know. They were the cries of a man who had been given his own life back by another father's daughter, another young woman who would never get married or bring a child into this too often unfair world. "Our daughter was killed young, too. I know what that feels like and I know what it meant to her parents to give up her organs. I found myself wondering, 'when is this gonna stop?' I was conscious of the connection between Kerri and the girl who gave her lungs to me — I was aware of the link between me and the father of the other girl."

After two days in the critical care unit, Dave's heart rate had stabilized enough for him to return to his sixth-floor room. The remorse and guilt, which had generated his crying spells, leveled off as well. Building in place of these unfamiliar emotions were Dave's natural grit and determination. "You need a certain attitude to go out in the bush and look for trouble as a Reconn Marine," explains Dave, "and you need a similar kind of toughness to be a lung transplant patient. In both worlds, you never know what's waiting for you around the corner, but your main goal is to survive. I knew that I needed to survive to take care of my family. Before my operation, the odds were against me being able to do that. But after the operation, as I felt my strength coming back, I began to like my odds."

Dr. Elbert Trulock, Dave's Barnes Hospital pulmonologist and a member of the lung transplant medical review team, recognized that quiet determination the first time he met the broad-shouldered beer hauler. “Dave was a man of few words,” Dr. Trulock recalls of his initial assessment of a patient who had lost 50 percent of his lung capacity, but none of his quiet perseverance. Dr. Trulock recognized quickly that a transplant would be Dave’s only hope. But did he have the physical, emotional, psychological and family support foundation to stand up to one of the most demanding medical procedures anyone can endure? “I thought right away that he would be a good candidate,” Dr. Trulock says. “Testing revealed no major medical problems, his liver and heart were in good shape. But just as importantly, it was evident to me that Dave had that solid base of family support that’s so important to long-term survivability. He had the psychosocial structure to succeed. On the surface, I could tell he was a man of great self-control and self-discipline — with the determination to get where he was going. Under the surface I could tell that he was concerned, but he came across as incredibly stoic.”

Dave’s Midwestern stoicism, his emotional shield of invincibility, had been deeply pierced by the transplant team who had opened up his chest like a car hood and replaced two nearly useless lungs with the fresh organs of a dead 15-year-old girl. The 18-inch scar that lines his upper torso, and the scars of loss tracing through his memories and dreams came together during those momentous days. His wife, and the rest of Dave's world, would come to know a fundamentally altered man. He was now a man glad to value the beauty of each moment alive, happy to feel each sensation at an instinctively deeper level than ever before. But in these first, frustrating days after his transplant, Dave's feelings evolved from fear and vulnerability to naked, driven determination. Dave had to survive. He had come too far.

Back in his room Dave's focus was taking one step at a time, literally. With the help of his nurses, initially, and then alone, he got out of bed to walk the sixth-floor hallways four times a day. He also practiced a deep coughing and back-thumping procedure called percussion to avoid the dangerous potential of fluid building up in his new lungs and causing pneumonia. Initially, shaky on his feet, Dave began to look forward to the tentative strolls. With each widening stride, he felt his strength rising back up from his feet into his body. The new lungs helped, of course, pushing a full volume of air into his chest and out into the rest of his body through his newly oxygen-infused bloodstream. As he walked down those halls, as he took each new breath, that ever present hope remained in the back of his mind. Would he make it and would he be strong enough to walk Krista down the aisle at her wedding.

Still Dave's appetite wasn't there yet, and worse there was his embarrassing inability to have a bowel movement. Like the other obstacles, Dave overcame this uncomfortable, painful distraction, primarily through the force of his own will, and within four days he was back on a small ration of solid food. Dave approached this aspect of his recovery — like everything else — with determination. "My sister Jean smuggled me in a chicken sandwich," he says, "and even though I wasn't very hungry, it felt like an achievement to get down something that wasn't coming out of an intravenous tube."

Dave's life-preserving medications were mixed, at first, in his milk or juice for ease of digestion. Dave had always considered himself an organized man. At times, in Vietnam, his life and his squad's existence had depended on his ability to keep complex orders and procedures straight. In his professional life he had found success, in part, through his God-given ability to manage detailed beer distribution plans and keep routes de-conflicted and in tact, pretty much in his own head. But now the correct order, dosage, timing and identification of multiple medications, like cyclosporine, would keep him alive. In the same way that Dave memorized communication codes as a Marine radioman, he now committed to instant recall a series of requirements for taking seven different medications twice daily. These pills were, from now on, his chief defense against infection, organ rejection and sure death. Just like in the Marines, he learned this vital lesson from a chart that hung on the wall — this time in a St. Louis hospital room instead of a San Diego Quonset Hut.

Despite losing about 20 pounds, Dave knew he was actually growing stronger. To keep his focus on recovery sharp, he declined the company of many visitors, except Judy, who sensed his emotional distance. “Although the long-term impact of his transplant was to make Dave much more emotional than he had ever been before, he closed down to me in those first few days after the surgery,” she recalls. “It was very upsetting, but I think now it his way of dealing with the enormity of what he had been through, and his need to keep his attention fixed on doing what he had to do to get better.”

Dave was achieving his goal. He was getting better quickly. “I got my first weekend pass to go home after nine days," he says with the bright smile of a sweet memory, a cherished victory. The oxygen canister was in the car just in case, but it was no longer a necessary appendage for Dave to breath normally. The Sikes pulled into Clara Sikes' 12-family East Belleville apartment complex. Dave honked the horn. He knew his mother was no fan of surprises, but he couldn't resist this gesture of precious independence. Getting out of the Ford, he tugged a bit at the staples in his chest. He sensed that he could distinguish each individual staple of the 163 clips that attached the two sides of his body above the waist. Despite that sensation, the successful double lung transplant patient felt more normal than he had felt in two years.

His mother, five-feet-tall, energetic, with short snow-white hair and clear blues eyes that reflected fierce German independence, had lost countless hours of sleep worrying about her sick son. She called him in the hospital every day, just as she had called or seen him most days of his life since the day in 1949 when the nuns brought him home to her from an East St. Louis hospital. She had no idea that he was coming home to her now on his own. She wished her husband, E.J., dead since 1977, could see this. Behind her spectacles, her eyes fill with tears as Clara watched her only son bounce up the eight stairs to her apartment.

Dave pushed away the realization that he would have to be back to his hospital room by 8 p.m. Sunday evening. It was only a weekend pass. At this moment, unlike endless previous moments, fading into months, where only waiting for the future held meaning, Dave was fully alive in the present. "It was so great to sit in the living room across from my mom, in my favorite big chair, simply breathing freely. "To be able to take a deep breath without breaking into a violent coughing spell, to be able to walk to the bedroom without taking my oxygen tank with me — felt like a miracle."

Later that night, Dave and Judy felt the miracle of lying once again in a bed in each other's arms. The couple was beginning to feel like human beings again. And even Dave's mandatory, and all-too-quick return to Barnes — the routine of daily medications and increasingly strenuous physical therapy — couldn't dampen their enthusiasm. "I had daily sessions on the treadmill at the hospital and I could really feel my lung capacity expanding," Dave says. "Four or five times a day I'd go down to X-ray to get the updated pictures of my lungs that my team needed to track my progress."

That straight-line progress was restrained slightly by a common virus, called CMV, which slowed down the anxious patient. Although his flu-like symptoms made him feel sluggish for the first time in days, strong antibiotics and his own determination quickly dispatched the bug. Dave continued to breath freely and his two healthy young lungs showed no signs of being rejected by his body. On the fifteenth day of his long hospital stay, Dave asked Dr. Trulock if he could go home. The answer was yes. In true, understated Dave Sikes style his response was "Thanks a lot."

On a Friday afternoon, Dave returned to his Millstadt, Ill., home. Judy and Jean Marie, Dave's sister, had fastened balloons and banners around the yard and front of the one-story brick, ranch-style house with detached two-car garage where the Sikes had lived for 17 years. Dave stood in the front yard and hugged Judy and Krista as tightly as his still diminished strength would allow him to hold on. He had been through hell, but now he had been reborn. He took a deep pull of crisp southern Illinois February air. He put his arm round Judy's shoulder gently, and they walked together toward the front door. He knew, as he walked through that door, that his new life had begun.

Krista & Randy get married, Novermber 11, 1995

Walk me down the aisle Daddy

Returning home, for the reborn Dave , was much more than simply resuming the familiar routines of life. His new lungs energized him at a pace that had not been seen around the Sikes' Millstadt home since the his days of beer hauling and racquetball. In fact, Dave's desire to return to the racquetball court, the golf course and his career were coveted goals that drove his comeback. "I was bound and determined to get back on my feet in every way," he says. "Sure, I wasn't quite as strong immediately after the transplant, but soon I was doing all those things."

Dave was on his way to a full recovery, but there were important interim steps along the way. Like rehabilitation at Barnes Hospital five days a week for three months. In the hospital's well-equipped rehab suite, the former Marine put himself through a grueling regimen that surpassed his basic training experience in physical intensity. "I'd work on my legs and endurance on the stationary bike and the treadmill, and then lift weights to build up my strength and get the power back in my arms," Dave recalls.

But it was the emotional muscles that Dave was developing, and exercising regularly, that most impressed his supportive bride. "He was like a new person — optimistic in a way he never was before, just happy to be alive," Judy says. "He was more emotional and in touch with his feelings. He might be watching TV and cry at a commercial, especially anything about a child."

Dave checked in regularly with Dr. Trulock, who was gratified, if not surprised, by Dave's steady progress. "Dave is doing as well as any of our recipients have," explains Dr. Trulock. He has no outward symptoms of lung rejection, and he has resumed an active recreational life and career. Dave, like all of our successful transplant patients, is more than just a metaphor for rebirth. He is living his life with a renewed commitment and sense of purpose."

Dave's determination to squeeze the most out of life is underwritten by sobering outcome data. Dr. Trulock explains that "transplant is treatment, not a cure. The risk of organ rejection is significant and an ongoing possibility," the physician adds, citing one of the few available studies for the relatively modern procedure. In that research, which followed patients from the groundbreaking Toronto program starting in the mid-

1980s, 50 percent of patients lived 5-10 years. The longest surviving lung transplant recipient recently passed the 14-year mark.

Though he is reluctant to discuss his own prospects for longevity, the 53-year-old 7-year transplant survivor takes great pride and comfort in the reality that he has already beaten the odds. "It's all about a higher purpose, he says with a smile. "What the transplant taught me — what my entire life has shown me — is there's more to life than just existing on Earth."

In the months following his surgery, Dave blossomed into a new state of health and activity that resembled his old active self. "I felt the best I've felt in my life — I was still alive," he says triumphantly. "I'd gone from a total lack of functioning to being able to take full, normal breaths every day. I really had the sense that somebody had given me a second chance."

Judy noticed an increased ability in her husband to shake off small setbacks and worries, while focusing on the everyday pleasures in his new life. The smell of a rack of freshly baked chocolate chip cookies, the twinkling notes of a newly mastered Christmas Carol he performed on his piano — these were the sensations that gave meaning and distinction to each new day. Those subtle achievements were mixed in with the solid satisfaction of gripping a golf club to play a real round only three months after the transplant.

Seven months after receiving his new lungs, Dave began a new career at a local trucking firm. "My job as a trucking operations manager was to sell our ability to move freight for a given amount of dollars," Dave says. "I had always had a very physical job, but the new person I was discovered that I enjoyed a job where I got to think more."

His rate of progress and his irrepressible attitude opened up another line of activity. Dave became Dr. Trulock's walking testimonial on the on the power and potential of successful lung transplantation. "My doctors couldn't believe my progress," Dave says with a smile and a shrug. "Dr. Trulock used me as an example to other patients." Dave's story was uplifting on many levels for the panels of eager lung transplant candidates who would sometimes confuse him with a physician because of his vibrant appearance, confident delivery and detailed clinical knowledge. Sometimes a prospective transplant recipient would call Dave at home to talk at length about his experience. On other occasions, Dave would accept a referral number and place the call himself. Judy would frequently hear a hearty laugh or even the broken cadence of Dave's cracking voice coming from her husband's favorite chair where he settled in to take the calls.

Along with frequent panel appearances and bi-monthly visits to see Dr. Trulock, Dave took his immune system-depressing medicine twice daily. Regular exercise, a healthy diet and plenty of sleep were routines that became second nature to the steadily stronger survivor. "It was a change in my lifestyle for the better," he explains. "The reality of existence as a transplant patient means you have to live healthier. The blood tests they took at the hospital told my doctors exactly how I was treating my body. Someone who might go out and have a couple of beers or smoke cigarettes would just be kidding themselves."

In addition to supporting potential transplant recipients at the hospital, the Sikes gladly took part in many events designed to advance the cause of donor and transplant awareness throughout the region. At events like a 1997 tree-planting ceremony in front of Barnes-Jewish Hospital, and a mass march in downtown St. Louis to the Arch, the Sikes shook hands, manned booths and enthusiastically signed up new organ donor volunteers. Dave even appeared in two public television commercials and an internal video for the Barnes-Jewish Hospital medical staff.

At a special donor awareness breakfast at St. Louis' ornate Roman Catholic Cathedral, Dave brought his own down-to-earth style to the presentation in a way that brought tears and lifted hearts. "I pretty much adlibbed my talk," he recalls. "I simply introduced myself and told the story of Kerri's death and my own rebirth through the miracle of my new lungs. You could have heard a pin drop in this audience of older men. These gentlemen — 10, 15, 20 years older than me were thinking: 'if he can go through that kind of ordeal, we can deal with the afflictions of old age that challenge us in our lives."

In addition to extensive local coverage in the *St. Louis Post Dispatch*, The *Belleville News Democrat*, area weekly newspapers and on radio and television stations, Dave ' story broke into the national spotlight when Judy sent her version of his story to *Good Housekeeping Magazine*. In the spring of 1997 Judy received a phone call at work. "This is the editor of Good Housekeeping and we'd like to publish your story," Judy recalls of the exciting message. After a phone interview with Dave and Judy, the magazine hired a contract photographer from St. Louis who came to the Sikes' Millstadt home and took what seemed to the couple to be hundreds of shots in their back yard. The article appeared in the May 1997 edition.

National television exposure was the next step on the Sikes' road to widescale advocacy of their donor awareness cause. When the producers of the Leeza Gibbons show saw the *St. Louis Post-Dispatch* version of his story reproduced on the Internet, a quick phone call followed. Airline tickets to Los Angeles, a hotel room and a limo ride to the studios brought Dave and Judy face to face with the opportunity to tell their story to millions of viewers around the country. Unfortunately, the sensational appetites of the daytime panel format did little justice to the poignant details of the Sikes real-life story.

As the last guests to appear more than an hour into the show, the Sikes were preceded by a segment on transplant survivors taking on the personalities of their donors and one on the unauthorized harvesting of donor organs. When perky Leeza finally asked the exhausted couple to describe the events around Kerri's death, Dave couldn't hold back the tears. Explains Judy: "When they began flashing pictures of Kerri on the monitors to tease the next segment we could tell that the purpose of the show was to generate emotion and not true awareness."

The price of Dave and Judy's newfound celebrity was a certain loss of privacy in the small community where they called home, but Dave considered that a price well worth paying. "I would be working with people on my job at the trucking firm and they would say, 'I know you. I just saw you on TV or in the newspaper.' I didn't mind talking to people. I believe in organ donation. And this is the only way to get the word out. If publicity like this helps save one person's life, it's worth the inconvenience."

In the aftermath of his lung transplant, Dave has accomplished many of his goals. He returned to work, returned to the golf course and returned to the level of intimacy and energy around his family that made life worth living for this proud survivor. But there was one key promise to be kept that, at Dave's darkest moments, had pushed him forward. He intended to walk his daughter Krista down the aisle at her wedding.

The wedding took place Nov. 11, 1995 at St. James Church in Millstadt where Kerri's funeral mass had been. The church was full as Dave escorted Krista down the aisle in her flowing white gown. The tears coursed down Dave's cheeks as he took one slow step after another, occasionally looking over at the veiled face of his daughter and smiling warmly. He knew that Kerri would have been so proud of her little sister. As the maid of honor she would have enjoyed her hunter green dress and ensuring that every detail went off without a hitch. He was in a tuxedo again for the first time since his own wedding.

"It was the happiest day of my life," Krista recalls. "Having my dad by my side to share this moment meant everything to me."

At the alter, Dave handed over his daughter to his son-in-law to be, Randy Clark. After a last kiss on Krista's cheek he slowly turned and took his seat beside Judy. He grasped his partner's warm hand. Alter candles blazed just above the head of the priest who was talking slowly to the smiling couple in front of him. Dave took a breath and closed his eyes slowly with the glow of the candles backlighting the images that danced from his memory into his thoughts.

A blonde, pigtailed girl clings to her daddy's arms as he holds her above the white, churning waves of the Pacific Ocean. Her pink shoulders are studded with gleaming white grains of sand and her clear, wide-open blue eyes match the ocean water above which she seems to soar like a gull. There is a small birthmark on her calf. She is giggling, squealing happily as the waves crash against the strong man's thick legs. She stops her squealing for an instant and points to the setting sun, an orange fireball sinking into the ocean on the faraway horizon. "Look Daddy, it's heaven," she tells her father, who holds her still above the water close to his chest and his beating heart. "That's right baby, that's where we'll all be together someday," he says. Slowly, he turns from the horizon and begins walking toward the shore and his young wife waving to them from the darkening beach.

Afterward

Dave has continued to overcome challenges in the eight years since he received his new lungs and his new, refocused life. At eight years, (he celebrated his transplant anniversary Feb. 8, 2003) he is one of the longest surviving patients in the Barnes-Jewish Hospital Lung Transplant Program. In that capacity he and Judy have taken every opportunity to serve as spokespeople and advocates for donor awareness and the transforming possibilities of organ transplantation. The Sikes have played a prominent role in marches, tree plantings, walking and running events, special days at the ballpark, and transplant picnics that bring together hundreds of transplant survivors.

Dave is well aware that the mortality rate for lung transplant recipients more than five years out from their surgery is more than 50 percent. That's the case even at a high-volume, world-renowned medical center like Barnes-Jewish Hospital and Washington University School of Medicine. "Life is very special and full right now and I plan to keep on living it to the fullest," says the determined former Marine.

Dave punctuates his words with a shaking, uplifted hand. He was diagnosed with Parkinson's disease in November 1998 which his doctors feel is unrelated to his transplant, and which has necessitated a complex new regimen of medicine, in addition to his anti rejection drugs. The Parkinson's has taken a toll physically. Although he is no longer able to work full-time, Dave tries to stay physically and emotionally engaged in an active life. He attends mass regularly with Judy at St. James Church in Millstadt, rehabs at his fitness club four to five times a week to keep his muscles from becoming more rigid, cooks meals and visits with his three grandchildren, Kerri, Cole & Kylie.

Kerri, the first of those grandkids, was born to Krista, now 29, and Randy in May 1997. The blonde-haired, blue-eyed youngster displays the energy and smile of her namesake, and a more unusual similarity. Kerri was born with a quarter-sized circular birthmark on the back of the calf of her left leg. It's identical to one that her aunt carried in the same place, says Judy . "We don't necessarily attach some kind of mystical meaning to that coincidence," Judy says, but we have always viewed our granddaughter as having a special link to the memory and spirit of our daughter."

In November 1998, Dave lost the only mother he has ever known. The loving woman who adopted him from St. Mary's Hospital in East St. Louis, Clara Sikes, passed away.

In 2002, Judy accepted a position as an assistant with the Breast Health Center at Barnes-Jewish Hospital, a job that places her in the midst of the caring medical community that she has come to know through Dave's experiences. She says her job at the hospital offers a new level of satisfaction and purpose.

As a couple, the Sikes' overriding purpose remains to deliver their message of hope and faith to as many people as possible. Their story has continued to receive local media attention, including recent updates in the St. Louis Post Dispatch, and on the local NBC television affiliate and the National Public Radio station. Dave continues to take part in the informational panels at Barnes-Jewish, where he role models an uplifting example to prospective lung transplant recipients and their families.

The future still appears open and promising to Dave and Judy. In 1998 they moved into the third home they've owned in Millstadt in their 18 years there. They dream today of new possibilities. Dreams mean something more when you receive a second chance at life, and when you're walking that journey with your soul mate. The publication of a book that would share their story and inspire thousands; wonderful holiday celebrations with Krista, Randy and the grandkids; the simple chance to hold one another for another moment, another day, another year.

The Sikes cherish all those hopes. But their greatest wish is this. That people they don't know, in the midst of adversity, at the darkest hour of their greatest challenge, will find hope and comfort in the story of an orphan who traveled far, suffered much, trusted God and came home finally to a new world where miracles happen every day.

www.ingramcontent.com/pod-product-compliance
Ingram Content Group UK Ltd.
Pitfield, Milton Keynes, MK11 3LW, UK
UKHW040015200726
13854UKWH00001B/211

9 781412 001496